SET B

Get Amer[illegible] Singing...Again!

Strategies for Teaching

Lesson Ideas and Activities for Meeting the Standards

By Loretta Mitchell Norgon

To Rob – thank you for your love and support

HAL•LEONARD®
CORPORATION
7777 W. Bluemound Rd. P.O. Box 13819 Milwaukee, WI 53213

Preface

Get America Singing...AGAIN,* the national campaign and collections of songs that every student should know and be able to sing, has made an impact on students' common repertoire. ***Strategies for Teaching (Set A)*** combined our common song repertoire from the original publication with teaching strategies to meet the National Standards. This publication, ***Strategies for Teaching (Set B)***, takes that process a step further, by providing teaching strategies for selected songs in ***Get America Singing...AGAIN Volume 2***. It can be used in addition to Set A, or on its own, along with the selected songs from Volume 2.

Using the same format as Set A, ***Strategies for Teaching (Set B)*** contains ready-to-use ideas for integrating essential repertoire into our everyday teaching. With these activities, teachers can work toward and achieve the National Standards.

The book contains ten sections, one for each of ten songs from ***Get America Singing...AGAIN Volume 2***. Each section features teaching ideas and learning activities, aligned specifically with one or more of the National Standards. The strategies are designed to integrate with national as well as local music standards.

Created for music specialists and classroom teachers from kindergarten through grade 8, each activity targets one or more levels. The reproducible pages can be duplicated to create transparencies or individual student copies. Student learning activities such as "Discovering Major and Minor," "A Gershwin Puzzler," "Composing Your Own Flag Song," and "Adding Orff," help students interact with the song material as they work toward the Standards.

Teacher instructions are designed to be user-friendly, providing the information that music teachers need most quickly and concisely. Each includes:

Grade Level(s):
National Standard(s)
Objective(s):
Materials:
Directions:

Use all of the ideas, or select the learning activities that fit the needs of your curriculum, your classroom and/or your own teaching style. Feel free to adapt, modify, and extend. You may wish to modify the difficulty level of some activities to meet the needs of students older or younger than those for whom the activity was intended. The suggestions may serve as a catalyst for your own ideas. Amplify the strategies with your own creative ways of using our common song repertoire for standards-based instruction.

I hope that this resource will help you incorporate more of America's favorite songs into your classroom as you help your students meet the National Standards.

Loretta Mitchell Norgon

*A Project of the Music Educators National Conference
Get America Singing...AGAIN! ©1996, And Get America Singing...AGAIN! Volume 2 ©2000, both published by Hal Leonard Corporation

Get America Singing...Again!

Strategies for Teaching (Set B)

Lesson Ideas and Activities for Meeting the Standards

Teacher Instructions

Camptown Races

Activity 1-1: About the Composer

Grade Level: 4-6
National Standard: 9

Objective
Students understand the origin and background of a song.

Materials
- Get America Singing…AGAIN! Volume 2, Singer's Edition, p. 9
- Student copies of 1-1
- Pencils
- Research materials or internet access

Directions
Open the class period by singing the song. Ask, "How many of you have heard this song before?" Facilitate a class discussion including any of the following:
- Where students have heard this tune
- What lyrics they recall
- What meaning they attach to the song

Distribute student copies of 1-1. Invite students to read individually or as a class as appropriate to students' reading abilities. Instruct students to work individually, in partners, or in small groups to find answers to the research questions. Encourage students to share their responses with the class.

Answer Key (Student Responses may include:)
1. *Foster's parents actually discouraged his interest in music, and would have preferred that he go into business instead.*
2. *"Swanee River" ("Old Folks at Home") - official state song of Florida. "My Old Kentucky Home" - state song of Kentucky.*
3. *"Oh, Susanna!"*

Activity 1-2: Playing the Chord Roots

Grade Level: 2-5
National Standard: 2

Objective
Students play chord roots to accompany a song.

Materials
- Get America Singing…AGAIN! Volume 2, Singer's Edition, p. 9
- Transparency and student copies of 1-2
- Mallet instruments or keyboards

Directions
Display a transparency of 1-2. Help students learn to play the chord roots using bells, keyboard, or other melodic instrument. Select students to play the chord roots as the class sings the song.

Activity 1-3: All Bottled Up

Grade Level: 3-5
National Standard: 2, 8

Objectives
- Students play chord roots to accompany a song.
- Students make connections between music and science.

Materials
- Get America Singing…AGAIN! Volume 2, Singer's Edition, p. 9
- Transparency and student copies of 1-3
- Empty soda bottles and water

Directions
Display a transparency of 1-3. Guide students to pour water into each of the three bottles to tune them to the pitches, D, A, and G. Ask "What are you noticing about the volume of water, compared to the pitch that we hear?" Help students learn to blow across the bottle openings to play the chord roots. Guide students as they follow the transparency and play the chord roots on the steady beat as the class sings the refrain.

Activity 1-4: Play Along

Grade Level: 1-3
National Standard: 2

Objective
Students perform patterns on melodic instruments.

Materials
- Get America Singing…AGAIN! Volume 2, Singer's Edition, p. 9
- Transparency of 1-4
- Student copies of Player #1 and Player #2 cards (cut apart)
- Mallet instruments or keyboards

Directions
Display the transparency of 1-4. Help students sing the icons and lyrics. Select two students to play the melody patterns on Player #1 and Player #2 cards. Sing the song with the class. Invite individuals to play along as their patterns occur. Guide the class to identify other (similar) occurrences of these patterns in the song. Sing the song again, inviting players to accompany the patterns as they occur.

Activity 1-5: Play the Rhythm

Grade Level: 2-3
National Standards: 2, 5

Objective
Students read icons and perform rhythmic patterns on classroom instruments.

Materials
- Get America Singing…AGAIN! Volume 2, Singer's Edition, p. 9
- Transparency or student copies of 1-5
- Classroom rhythm instruments

Directions
Display the transparency or distribute student copies of 1-5. Help students read the icons and lyrics with accurate rhythm. Select individual students to play each pattern. Sing the song with the class. Invite individuals to play along as each pattern occurs. Perform the entire song again. Select other students to play as the class sings.

Activity 1-6: Rhythm Canon

Grade Level: 4-7
National Standards: 2, 5

Objectives
- Students read traditional notation and perform rhythmic patterns on classroom instruments.
- Students perform a rhythm canon.

Materials
- Get America Singing…AGAIN! Volume 2, Singer's Edition, p. 9
- Transparency and student copies of 1-6
- Classroom rhythm instruments

Directions
Display the transparency or distribute student copies of 1-6. Help students to read the patterns and lyrics with accurate rhythm. Select individual students to play each pattern. Sing the song with the class. Invite individuals to play along as each pattern occurs. Perform the song again. Select other students to play as the class sings. To perform a canon, divide the class into four groups, and distribute instruments to each group as indicated. Perform the four patterns in sequence, first, in unison, and then as a canon, inviting groups 2, 3, and 4 to listen for Group 1, and begin at the top, as Group 1 progresses through the patterns. If time permits, exchange instruments and perform the canon again.

Activity 1-7: Question and Echo

Grade Level: 3-5
National Standard: 3

Objective
(In preparation for improvisation), students respond to musical questions with musical echoes.

Materials
- Get America Singing…AGAIN! Volume 2, Singer's Edition, p. 9
- Transparency and student copies of 1-7

Directions
Introduce the concept of question and echo by inviting the class to "copycat" everything you say, e.g., "Hello. How are you?" – "Hello. How are you?" Display the transparency or distribute student copies of 1-7. Using speaking voices, practice question and echo, using phrases on the chart. Perform the question and echoes again, using singing voices. Be sure students understand that, it is not about the lyrics, but rather the musical elements that make the question and echo identical. To illustrate and reinforce, repeat the question and echo exercise omitting the lyrics - singing the melodies on a neutral syllable.

Activity 1-8: Question and Answer

Grade Level: 3-5
National Standard: 3

Objective
(In preparation for improvisation), students respond to musical questions with musical answers.

Materials
- Get America Singing…AGAIN! Volume 2, Singer's Edition, p. 9
- Transparency and student copies of 1-8

Directions
Review the concept of question and echo by repeating "copycat" exercise, e.g., "Hello. How are you?" – "Hello. How are you?" Introduce the concept of musical answers. Invite students to change their echoes to answers, e.g., "Hello. How are you?" – "Hello, I am fine." Display the transparency or distribute student copies of 1-8. Using speaking voices, practice question and answers, using the phrases on the chart. Perform the question and answers again, using singing voices. Be sure students understand that, it is not about the lyrics, but, rather the musical elements that make-up a question and answer. To illustrate and reinforce, repeat the question and answer exercise omitting the lyrics - singing the melodies on a neutral syllable.

Camptown Races

About the Composer

An American composer, Stephen Foster composed more than 200 songs in a very short lifetime. (He died at the young age of 37.) It is said that, at the age of two, he may have been already showing signs of his musical talent. As a child, he started playing the flute and the piano, and wrote his first song as a young teenager. He was known for creating new melodies whenever he picked up an instrument or sat down at a piano.

Foster's music grew out of his love for songs of the African-American people and work songs that he heard as a young boy. His beautiful melodies may give listeners a vision of life in the South in the middle 1800s. Some of his best-known works include "Camptown Races," "Oh! Susanna," "My Old Kentucky Home," "Jeannie with the Light Brown Hair," "Beautiful Dreamer," and "Old Folks at Home."

Questions for Discussion

1. How did Stephen's parents feel about his chosen profession?

2. Which of Foster's songs are the official songs of two of the 50 states?

3. Which of Foster's songs became the theme song of the 1849 California Gold Rush?

Camptown Races

Playing the Chord Roots

This song uses only three chords.

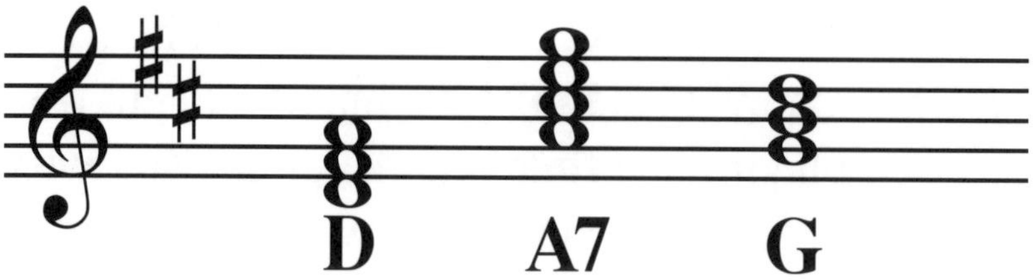

The chords contain these pitches:

D	A7	G
	G	
A	E	D
F♯	C♯	B
D	A	G

Each chord gets its name from the lowest pitch:
the ROOT of the chord.

Play these chord roots as your class sings "Camptown Races".
Watch a conductor or the music to know when to play each pitch.

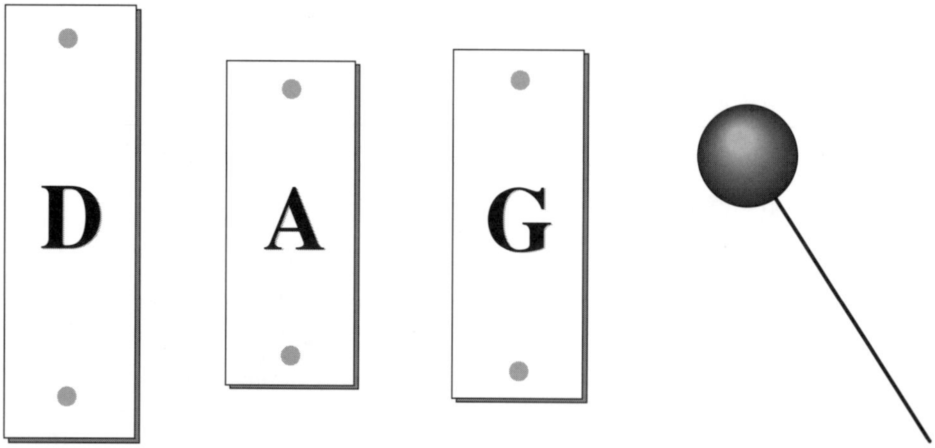

Camptown Races

All Bottled Up

Tune three bottles. Blow across the top of each bottle. Add water until the pitch matches the D, A, or G bell.

Blow across the bottles to play these chord roots as your class sings the refrain of "Camptown Races." Play one chord root on each heavy beat to accompany the refrain.

	D	D	D	D	G	G	D	D
	Goin' to	run all	night	-	Goin' to	run all	day.	-
	D	D	D	D	A	A	D	D
I'll	bet my	money on the	bob-tail	nag;	Some-body	bet on the	bay.	-

Camptown Races

Play Along

Directions: Find these bells. Play along with the song.

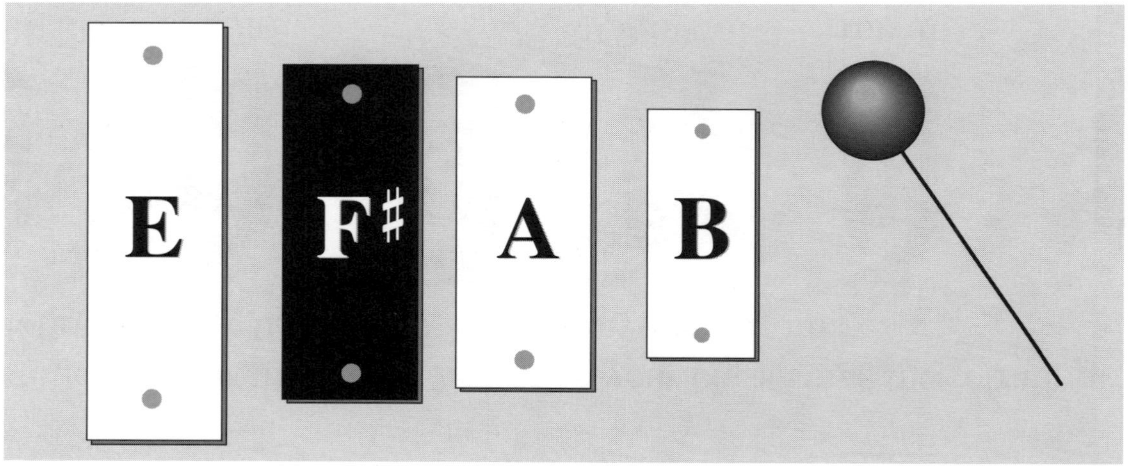

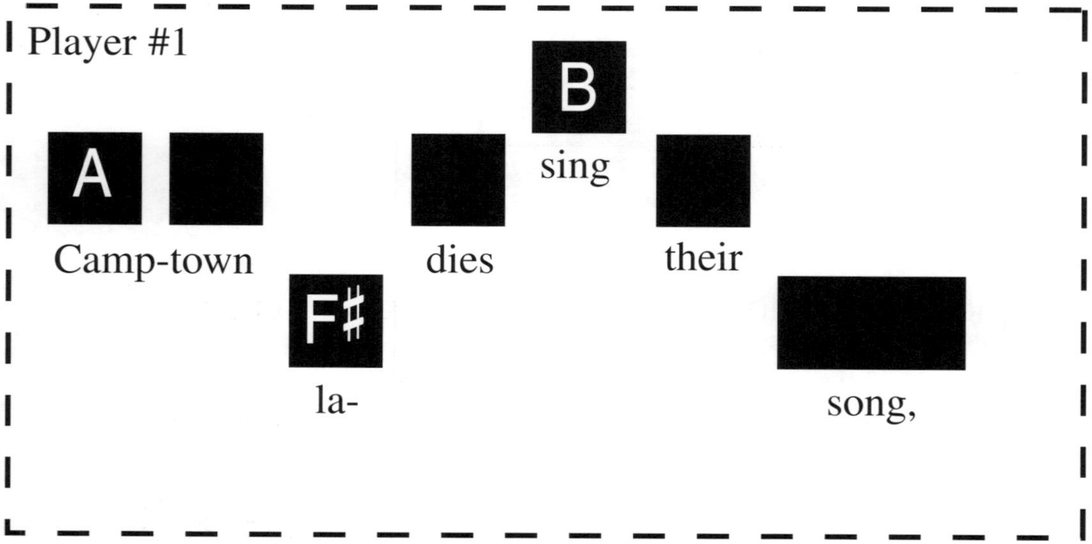

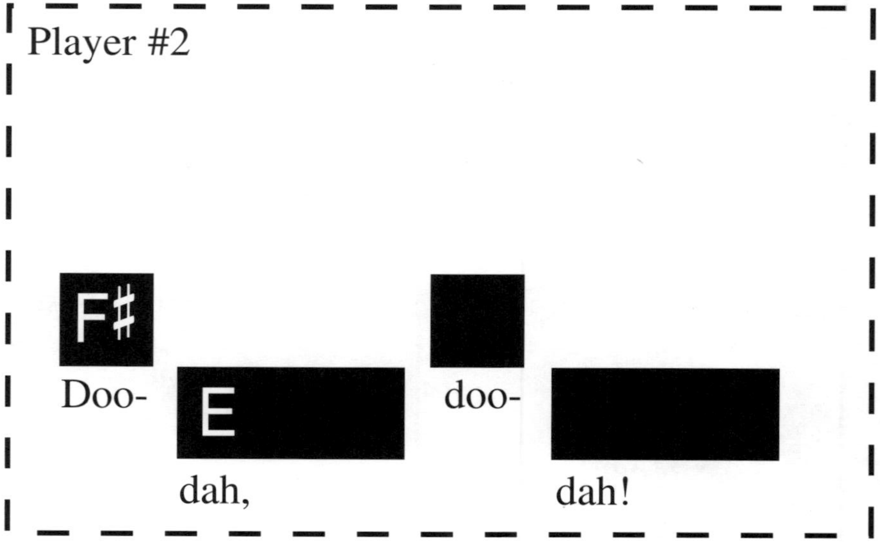

Camptown Races

Play the Rhythm

Directions: Choose an instrument. Read and play the rhythm patterns.

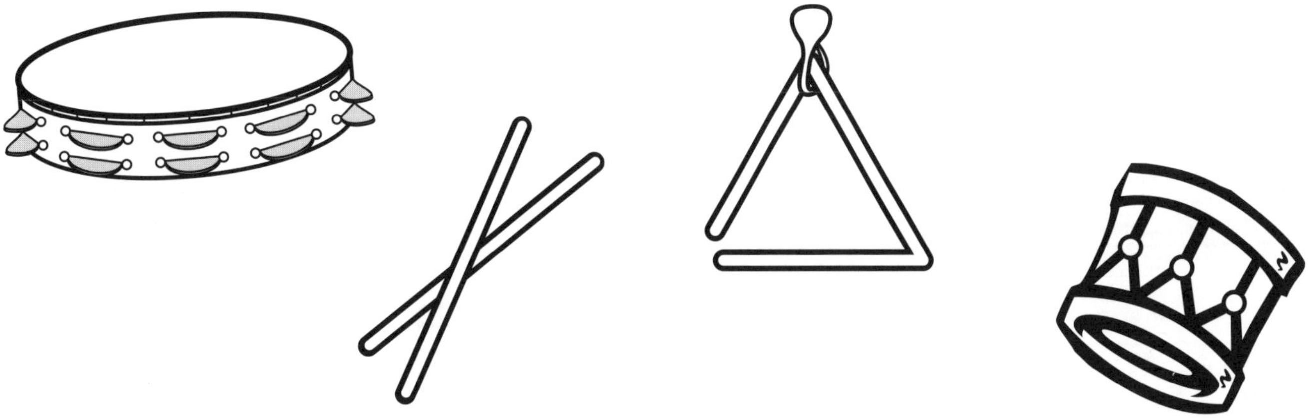

① 

Camp - town la - dies sing their song

② 

Bet my mon-ey on a bob - tail nag

③ 

Come down there with my hat caved in

④ 

Go back home with a pock-et full of tin

Camptown Races

Rhythm Canon

Directions: Choose an instrument. Read and play the rhythm patterns. Divide the class into four groups. Perform as a canon.

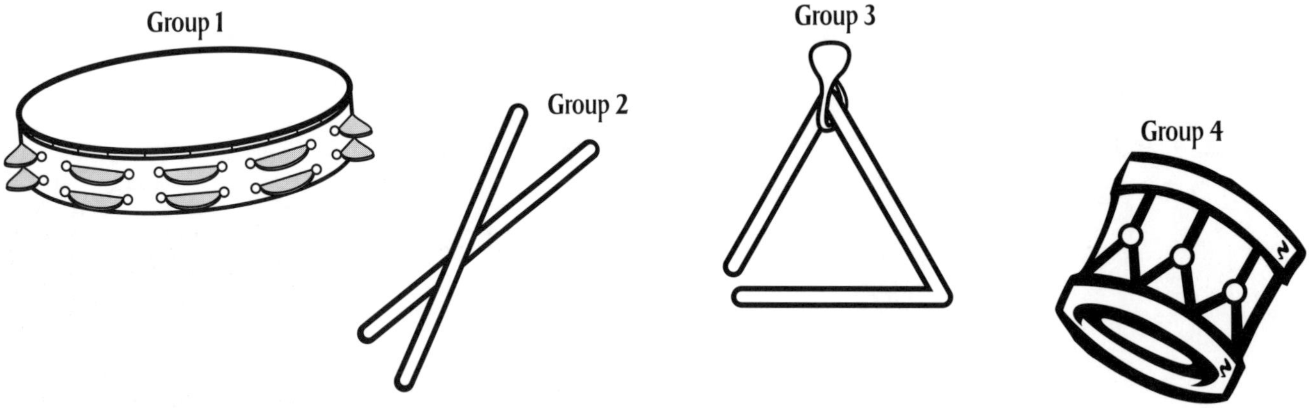

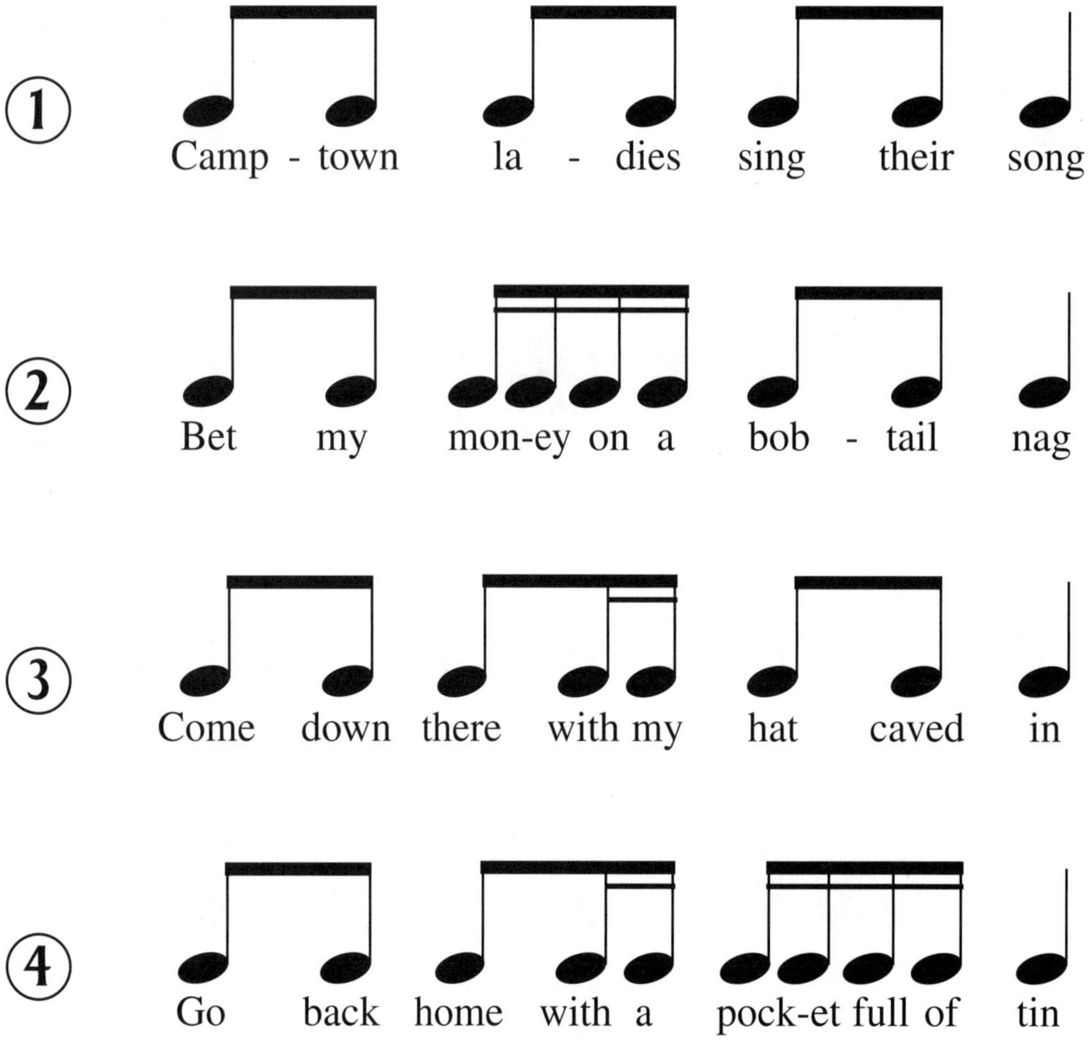

Camptown Races

Question and Echo

Directions: Listen to the leader. Respond to each question with an echo.

Question	Echo
Question and echo are exactly the same.	
Camptown ladies sing their song, doo-dah, doo-dah.	Camptown ladies sing their song, doo-dah, doo-dah.
I come down there with my hat caved in, doo-dah, doo-dah.	I come down there with my hat caved in, doo-dah, doo-dah.
The longtail filly and the big black horse, doo-dah, doo-dah.	The longtail filly and the big black horse, doo-dah, doo-dah.
The blind horse stickin' in a big mudhole, doo-dah, doo-dah.	The blind horse stickin' in a big mudhole, doo-dah, doo-dah.

Camptown Races

Question and Answer

Directions: Listen to the leader. Respond to each question with an answer.

Question	Answer
Question and answer start the same (musically). but **end differently...**	
Camptown ladies sing their song, doo-dah, doo-dah.	The camptown racetrack's five miles long. Oh, doo-dah day!
I come down there with my hat caved in, doo-dah, doo-dah.	I go back home with a pocket full of tin. Oh, doo-dah day!
The longtail filly and the big black horse, doo-dah, doo-dah.	They fly the track and they both cut across. Oh, doo-dah day!
The blind horse stickin' in a big mudhole, doo-dah, doo-dah.	Can't touch bottom with a ten-foot pole. Oh, doo-dah day!

Teacher Instructions

Down in the Valley

Activity 2-1: Singing with Syllables • Adding the Lyrics

Grade Level: 3-6
National Standards: 1, 5

Objective
Students read syllables and sing a traditional song

Materials
- Get America Singing...AGAIN! Volume 2, Singer's Edition, p.11
- Transparency or student copies of 2-1

Directions
Display the transparency or distribute student copies of 2-1. Assuming prior experience with solfege, assist students as they read and sing the song with syllables. Repeat the song, using the lyrics.

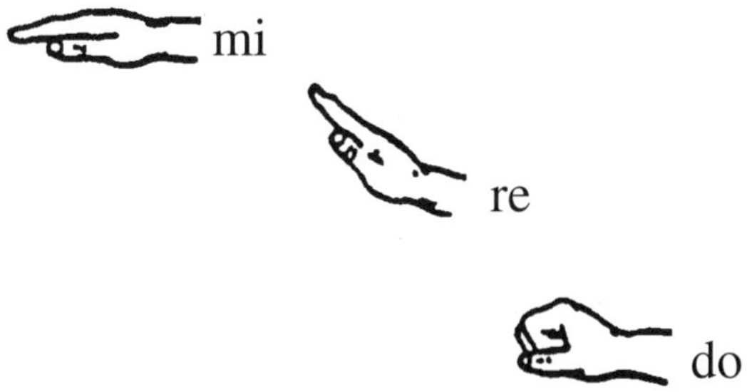

Activity 2-2: Singing with Hand Signs

Grade Level: 3-6
National Standards: 1, 5

Objective
Students read syllables and sing a traditional song.

Materials
- Get America Singing...AGAIN! Volume 2, Singer's Edition, p. 11
- Transparency or student copies of 2-2

Directions
Display the transparency or distribute student copies of 2-2. Assuming prior experience with Curwen/Kodály hand signs, assist students as they read and sing the song with syllables and signs.

Activity 2-3: Twos or Threes

Grade Level: 3-6
National Standard: 6

Objective
Students identify duple and triple meter in familiar songs.

Materials
- Get America Singing…AGAIN! Volume 2, Singer's Edition, p. 11
- Transparency and student copies of 2-3
- Pencils
- (Optional) recordings of "Happy Birthday," Twinkle Twinkle, Little Star," "America," "Yankee Doodle," and "Down in the Valley."

Directions
Begin the class with a review of duple and triple meter, (e.g., movement activity or hand jive). Distribute student copies of 2-3. Invite students to listen to "Happy Birthday," (recording, piano, recorder, or teacher's singing voice). Suggest that students pay particular attention to the patterns they hear, either strong-weak, or strong-weak-weak, and mark an "X" in the appropriate space. Continue with the other examples on the page, ending with "Down in the Valley."

Answer Key 1. 3s, 2. 2s, 3. 3s, 4. 2s, 5. 3s

Activity 2-4: Moving in Threes

Grade Level: 3-6
National Standard: 6

Objective
Students listen, follow, and describe triple meter.

Materials
- Get America Singing…AGAIN! Volume 2, Singer's Edition, p. 11
- Transparency and student copies of 2-4
- (Optional) recording of "Down in the Valley."
- Pencils

Directions
Begin the class with a review of duple and triple meter, (e.g., movement activity or hand jive.) Distribute student copies of 2-4. Invite students to listen to "Down in the Valley," (recording, piano, recorder, or teacher's singing voice). As students focus on the meter of the song, invite them to follow the "1-2-3" patterns with a pencil point. Invite the class to sing along as they repeat the activity.

Activity 2-5: Recorder Harmony

Grade Level: 3-6
National Standards: 2, 5

Objective
Students play a recorder duet.

Materials
- Get America Singing…AGAIN! Volume 2, Singer's Edition, p. 11
- Student copies of 2-5
- Recorders

Directions
Note transposition to key of G Major. Distribute student copies of 2-5. Divide class into two groups. Assist one group in learning the melody. Assist the other group in learning to play the harmony part. Pair each student with a partner and allow time for the partners to rehearse their duets. Encourage duets to perform for the class. Reassemble the groups, and work with each group to help them learn the opposite part. Pair with partners again. Allow time for practice, and more performances.

Activity 2-6: Find the Home Tones

Grade Level: 1-2
National Standard: 6

Objective
Students respond to prominent musical characteristics (home tone) while listening to music.

Materials
- Get America Singing…AGAIN! Volume 2, Singer's Edition, p. 11
- Transparency and student copies of 2-6
- F resonator bell and mallet (or other melodic instrument)

Directions
Display transparency of 2-6. Sing the song with the class. Use the transparency to focus students' attention on the occurrences of the F pitch throughout the song. Invite students to point out the Fs on the page and circle them. As the class sings the song, invite one student to play the Fs as they occur. As you complete the page, focus a discussion on the significance of the home tone.

Activity 2-7: Hand Jive

Grade Level: 2-4
National Standard: 6

Objective
Students demonstrate a triple meter.

Materials
- Get America Singing...AGAIN! Volume 2, Singer's Edition, p. 11
- Transparency and student copies of 2-7

Directions
Display transparency. With students, sing the song as your point to the illustrations to demonstrate the strong-weak-weak meter of the song. Distribute student copies of 2-7. As the class sings the song, help students point to the illustrations to identify and feel the meter in threes. Finally, help students create a hand jive that moves in patterns of threes, e.g, Pat knee 3X, Clap 3X, Right hand finger snap 3X, Left hand finger snap 3X.

Activity 2-8: Reading Dotted Half Notes

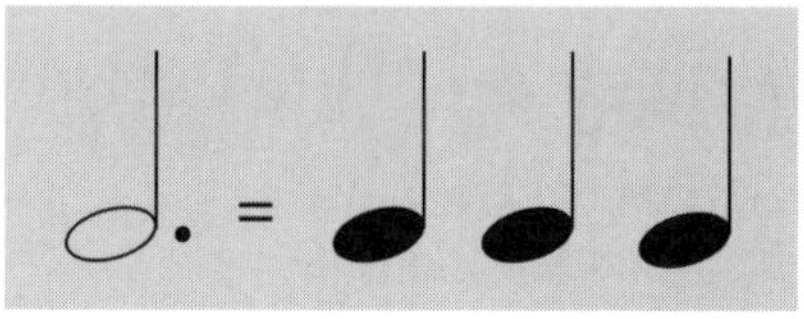

Grade Level: 3-6
National Standard: 5

Objective
Students read dotted half notes in 3/4 meter.

Materials
- Get America Singing...AGAIN! Volume 2, Singer's Edition, p. 11
- Transparency and student copies of 2-8

Directions
Display transparency. With students, chant rhythm syllables as you point to the illustration. Distribute student copies of 2-8. As the class works through the directions on the page, help individual students to identify and be able to read and perform dotted half notes accurately.

Down in the Valley

Singing With Syllables • Adding the Lyrics

Directions: Sing this song with syllables. Sing again using the lyrics.

sol do re mi do mi re do re
Down in the val- ley, val- ley, so low,

sol ti re fa re ti do re do
Hang your head o- ver, hear the wind blow

Down in the Valley

Singing with Hand Signs

Directions: Sing this melody using syllables. Use hand signs for sol, do, re, and mi, ti, and fa.

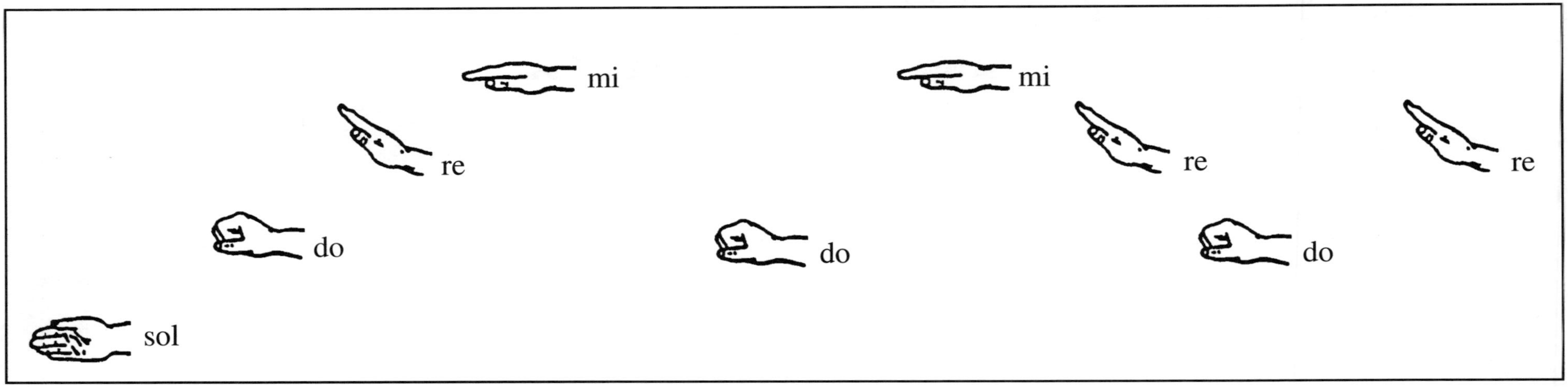

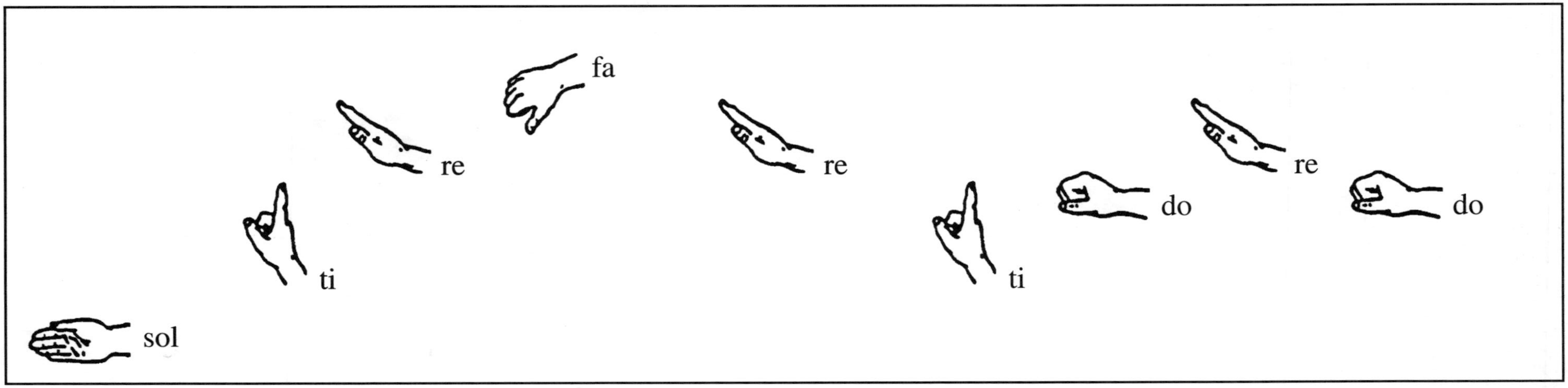

Down in the Valley

Twos or Threes

Directions: Listen for patterns of twos or threes, and mark your answer with an X in the box.

1. Happy Birthday 	☐ TWOs 1 2 1 2 1 2	☐ THREEs 1 2 3 1 2 3
2. Twinkle Twinkle, Little Star 	☐ TWOs 1 2 1 2 1 2	☐ THREEs 1 2 3 1 2 3
3. America 	☐ TWOs 1 2 1 2 1 2	☐ THREEs 1 2 3 1 2 3
4. Yankee Doodle 	☐ TWOs 1 2 1 2 1 2	☐ THREEs 1 2 3 1 2 3
5. Down in the Valley 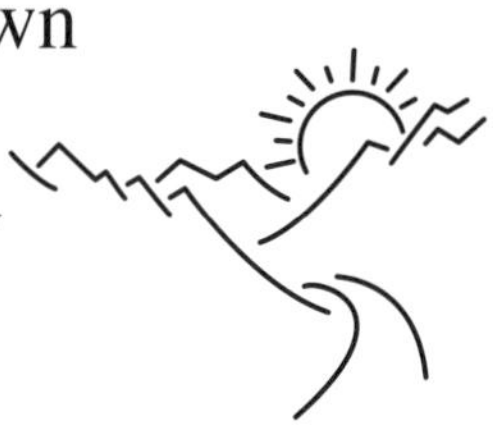	☐ TWOs 1 2 1 2 1 2	☐ THREEs 1 2 3 1 2 3

Down in the Valley

Moving in THREEs

Directions: Follow the Strong-Weak-Weak pattern as you sing this somg.

1 23 1 23 1 23 1 23 1 23 1 23

1 23 1 23 1 23 1 23 1 23

Down in the Valley

Recorder Harmony

Traditional Melody
Harmony by Loretta Norgon

Down in the Valley

Find the Home Tones

Directions: This song is written in the key of F Major. The name of the home tone will be F. Find all the home tones and circle them. As your class sings the song, play the home tones on a mallet instrument, wind instrument, or keyboard.

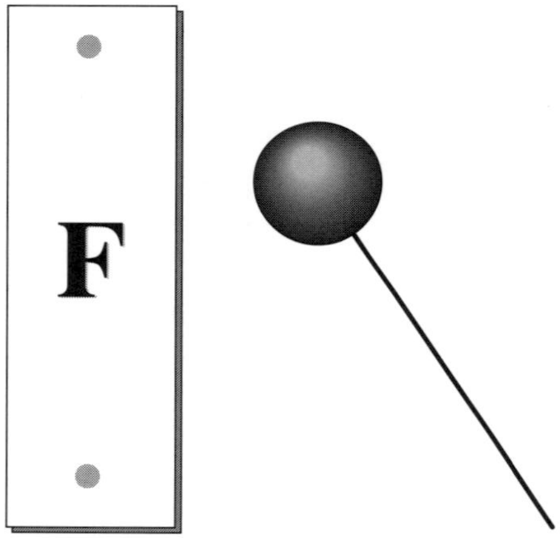

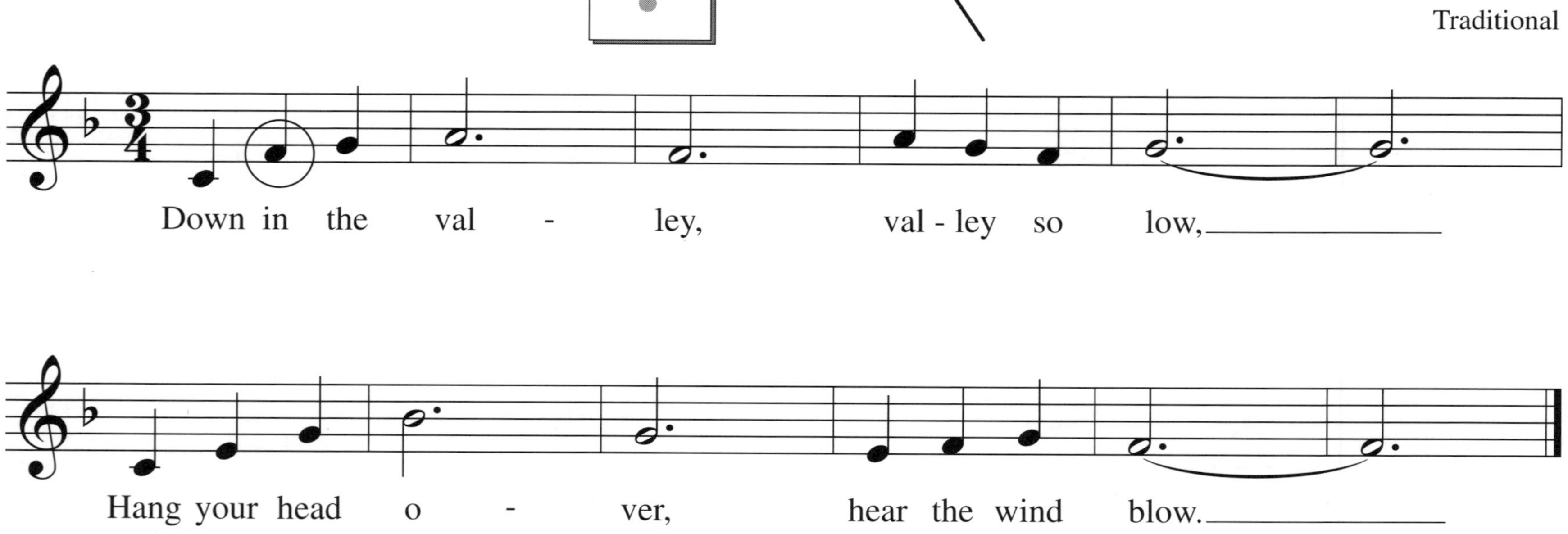

Down in the Valley

Hand Jive

Directions: As you sing this song, perform a hand jive by lightly tapping your toe and clapping. Then create your own hand jive that moves in threes.

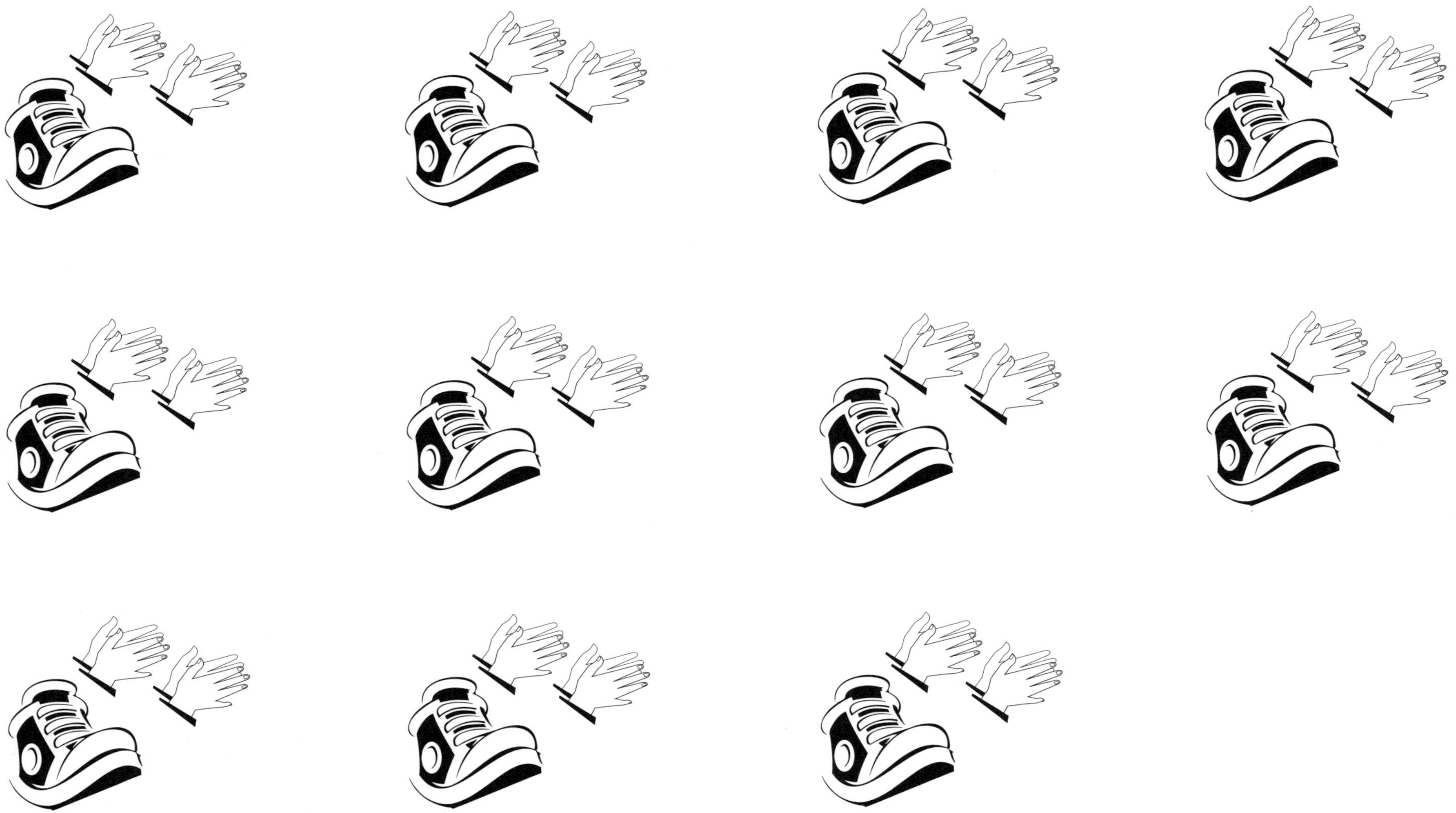

Down in the Valley

Reading Dotted Half Notes

Quarter Notes and Half Notes

Clap and chant:

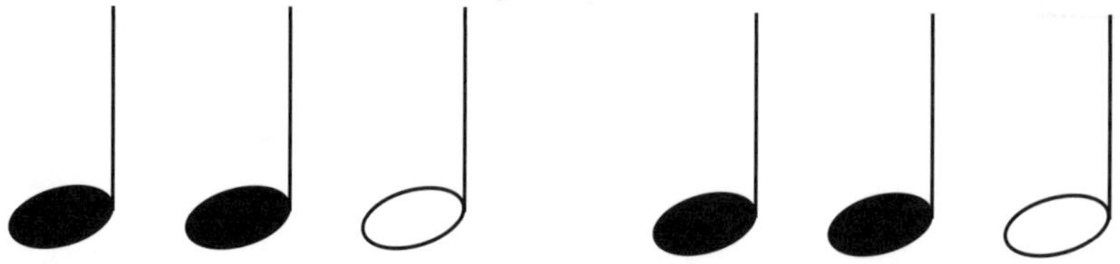

ta ta ta - a ta ta ta - a

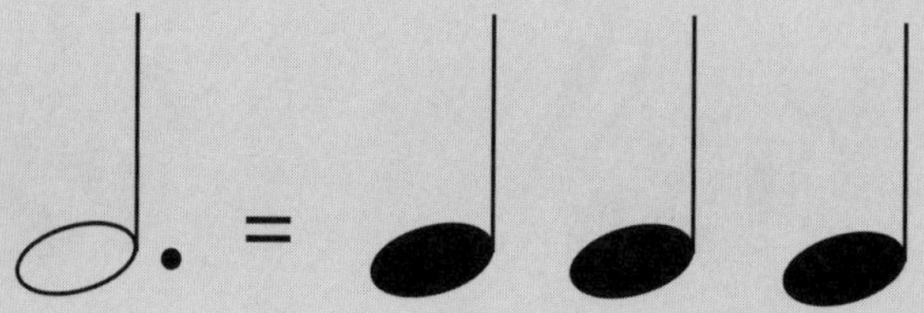

Quarter Notes and Dotted Half Notes

Clap and chant:

ta ta ta ta - a - a ta ta ta ta - a - a

From "Down in the Valley"

Clap and chant:

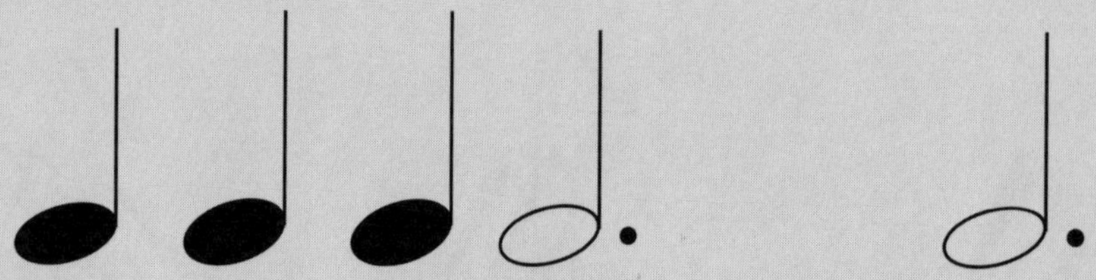

ta ta ta ta - a - a ta - a - a

Down in the val - ley

The Erie Canal

Activity 3-1: X Marks the Spot

Grade Level: 4-6
National Standard: 8

Objective
Students make connections between social studies and music.

Materials
- Get America Singing…AGAIN! Volume 2, Singer's Edition, p. 13
- Transparency or student copies of 3-1
- Research materials or internet access

Directions
Distribute student copies of 3-1. Instruct students to work individually, in partners, or in small groups to find and record responses to the research questions. Encourage students to share their responses with the class.

Answer Key (Student Responses may include:)
1. Albany, Buffalo, Schenectady
2. See map
3. See map
4. See map

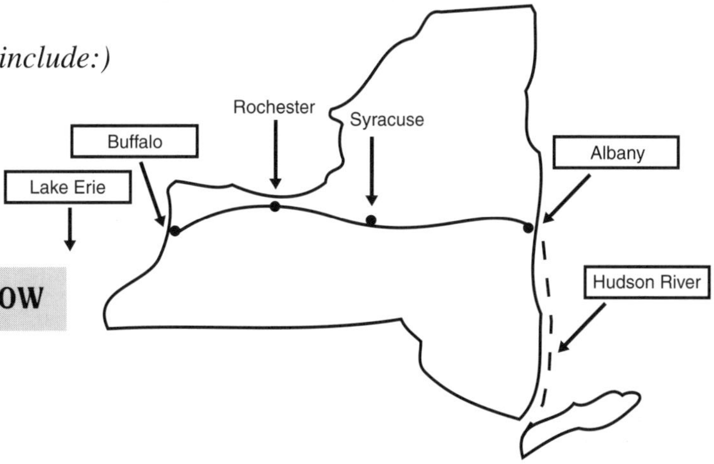

Activity 3-2: Show What You Know

Grade Level: 5-8
National Standard: 1, 9

Objective
Students understand the origin and background of songs in their varied repertoire.

Materials
- Get America Singin…AGAIN! Volume 2, Singer's Edition, p. 13
- Student copies of 3-2
- Pencils
- Research materials or internet access

Directions
Distribute student copies of 3-2. Instruct students to work individually, in partners, or in small groups to research and complete the activity page. Debrief the activity by encouraging students to share their responses with the class.

Answer Key (Student Responses may include:)
Vocabulary Builder
Canal – man-made waterway for travel
Lock – section of a canal with gates to let water in and out
Elevation – height above sea level
Barge – boat used to haul freight

Activity 3-3: Discovering Major and Minor

Grade Level: 4-8
National Standard: 6

Objective

Students use appropriate terminology (Major/Minor) in explaining music and music notation.

Materials

- Get America Singing…AGAIN! Volume 2, Singer's Edition, p. 13
- Student copies of 3-3
- Pencils
- Bells or keyboard(s)

Directions

Begin the class review of major and minor. Distribute student copies of 3-3. In partners, small groups, or as a whole class, follow directions on the page to discover examples of major and minor melody fragments in the song. Sing the song, paying particular attention to the major and minor sections.

Activity 3-4: Listening for Major and Minor

Grade Level: 3-6
National Standard: 6

Objective

Students listen and identify major and minor.

Materials

- Get America Singing…AGAIN! Volume 2, Singer's Edition, p. 13
- Transparency and student copies of 3-4
- Pencils
- Bells or keyboard

Directions

Begin the class with a review of major and minor (e.g. 3-3). Distribute student copies of 3-4. On bells or keyboard, play F major and d minor triads and fragments of F major and d minor melodies. Suggest that students pay particular attention to the tonality they hear, either major or minor, and mark an "X" in the appropriate space. Include fragments from the major and minor sections of "The Erie Canal." (The melody begins in d minor and changes to F major in the faster section – "low bridge".)

Activity 3-5: Dotted Eighths

Grade Level: 3-6
National Standards: 2, 5

Objective
Students read and perform patterns containing dotted eighth and sixteenth notes.

Materials
- Get America Singing...AGAIN! Volume 2, Singer's Edition, p. 13
- Transparency and student copies of 3-5
- Pencils

Directions
Display transparency. With students, chant rhythm syllables as you point to the illustration. Distribute student copies of 3-5. Guide students to follow the directions on the page, clapping and chanting rhythm syllables as printed (or other system as preferred by the teacher) for eighth, dotted eighth, and sixteenth notes.

Activity 3-6: Even or Uneven

Grade Level: 3-6
National Standard: 5

Objective
Students read and perform even and uneven rhythms.

Materials
- Get America Singing...AGAIN! Volume 2, Singer's Edition, p. 13
- Transparency and student copies of 3-6
- Wood block or other classroom rhythm instrument

Directions
Begin the class with a review of dotted eighth notes (e.g. 3-5). Distribute student copies of 3-6. Play short rhythm patterns containing even eighth notes and dotted eighth-sixteenth combinations. Suggest that students listen for even and uneven patterns and mark an "X" in the appropriate space. Include rhythm fragments from the song "The Erie Canal."

Activity 3-7: Similar and Different

Grade Level: 3-6
National Standard: 6

Objective

Students identify simple music forms.

Materials

- Get America Singing...AGAIN! Volume 2, Singer's Edition, p. 13
- 2 transparency copies of 3-7 (Keep one copy intact. Cut the boxes on the second copy apart.)

Directions

Display transparency of 3-7. Guide students to sing through the first two phrases on the page, and note the similarities. Using the cutouts, place the cutouts of phrases #1 and #2 on top of each other, to illustrate the melodic similarities. Use the transparency cutouts to illustrate contrasts in the third section. As you progress to the final section on the page, note similarities again. Help students discover a basic AABA form. Sing the song, helping students illustrate the AABA form with movement.

Activity 3-8: Create Your Own AABA

Grade Level: 3-6
National Standard: 4

Objective

Students compose in AABA form.

Materials

- Get America Singing...AGAIN! Volume 2, Singer's Edition, p. 13
- Transparency and student copies of 3-8
- Bells or keyboards

Directions

Review AABA form. Distribute student copies of 3-8. Divide students into groups, and instruct them to follow directions as printed to create an A section and a B section. Allow time for groups to create and practice their A and B sections and then combine them in AABA sequence. Invite groups to volunteer to perform their compositions for the teacher or for the class.

The Erie Canal

X Marks the Spot

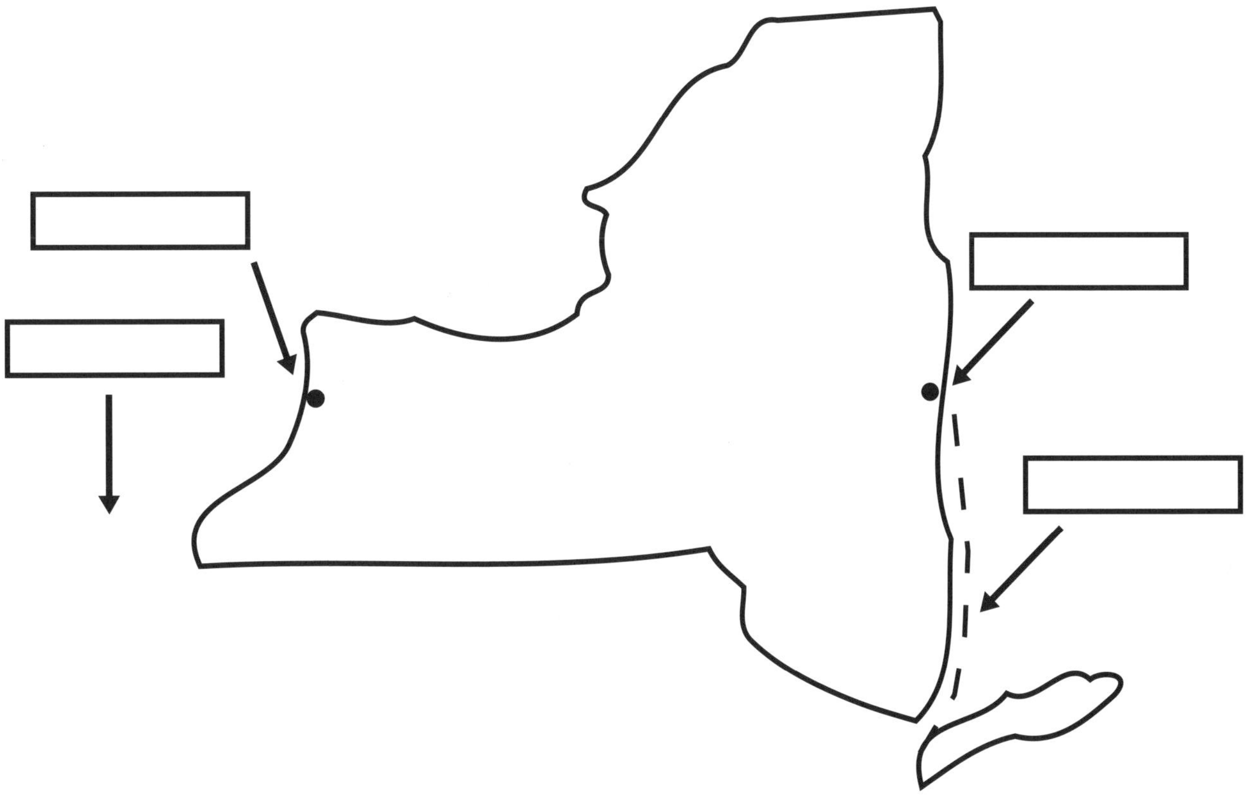

Questions to Research

1. What New York cities are mentioned in the song "The Erie Canal?"
2. Look up a map of the State of New York. Identify the following and write each name in the appropriate box on the map.
   - ☐ Albany
   - ☐ Buffalo
   - ☐ Lake Erie
   - ☐ Hudson River
3. Look up the route that the Erie Canal followed. Draw a line across the map to represent the canal's route.
4. What other cities are located along the route of the canal? Add their names to the map.

The Erie Canal

Show What You Know

Name________________________________ Class__________ Date________

Research and write your answers to the following questions:

1. Write a short paragraph about the Erie Canal.

____

____

____

____

____

____

2. Draw a diagram and label the parts to illustrate how locks work to make canal travel possible.

Vocabulary Builder

What do these words mean? Discuss these terms with your group. Look up the ones you do not know. Agree on a definition for each and write it in the blank.

canal ____

lock ____

elevation ____

barge ____

The Erie Canal

Discovering Major and Minor

Listen to the first few pitches of "The Erie Canal." These pitches outline a minor triad, the d minor chord. This song begins in the **key of D minor**.

D minor harmony is based on the pitches of the D minor scale.

- Play this scale on bells or keyboard.
- Circle the pitches that make up the **D minor triad.**

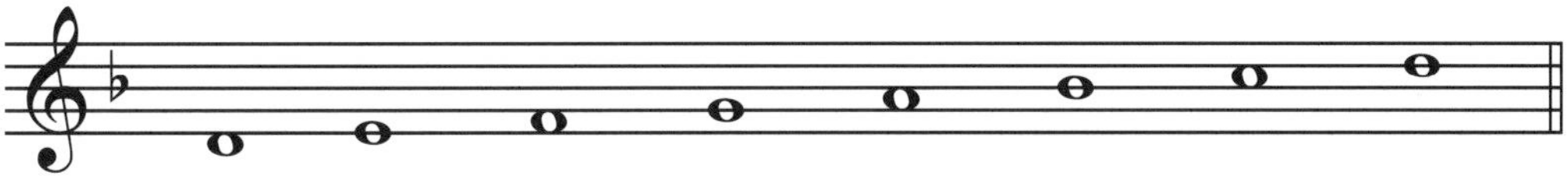

About 2/3 of the way through the song, the tonality changes. Listen to the harmony which appears with the following pitches. The tonality has changed to a major key: **the key of F Major**.

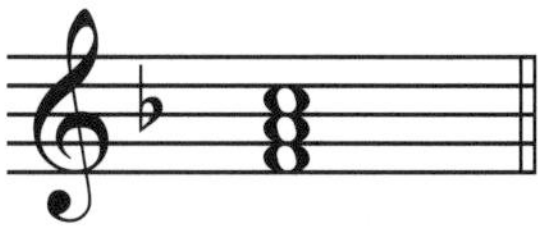

F Major harmony is based on the pitches of the F Major scale.

- Play this scale on bells or keyboard.
- Circle the pitches that make up the **F Major triad.**

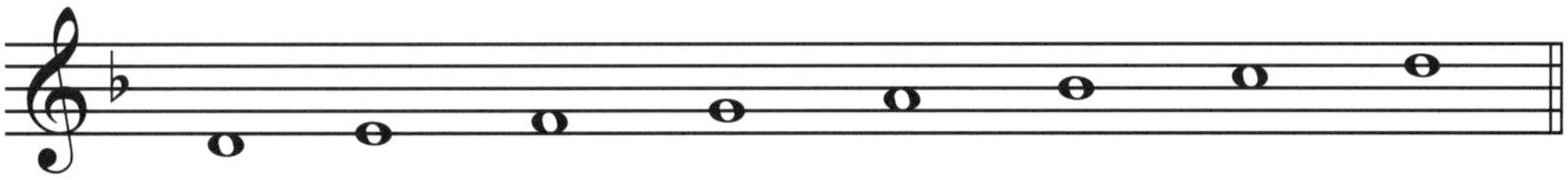

The Erie Canal

Listening for Major and Minor

Directions: Listen for F Major or D minor in the following examples. Mark your answer with an X in the box.

1.	**F Major** ☐ F A C	**D minor** ☐ D F A
2.	**F Major** ☐ F A C	**D minor** ☐ D F A
3.	**F Major** ☐ F A C	**D minor** ☐ D F A
4.	**F Major** ☐ F A C	**D minor** ☐ D F A
5.	**F Major** ☐ F A C	**D minor** ☐ D F A

The Erie Canal

Dotted Eighths

Eighth Notes and Sixteenth Notes

Chant and Play:

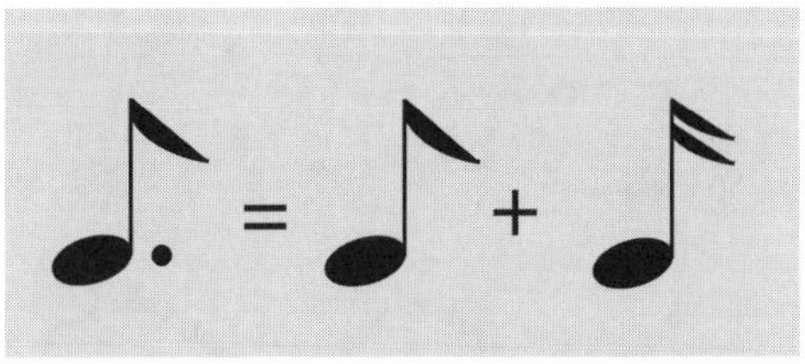

Dotted Eighth Notes and Sixteenth Notes

From "The Erie Canal"

Chant and Play:

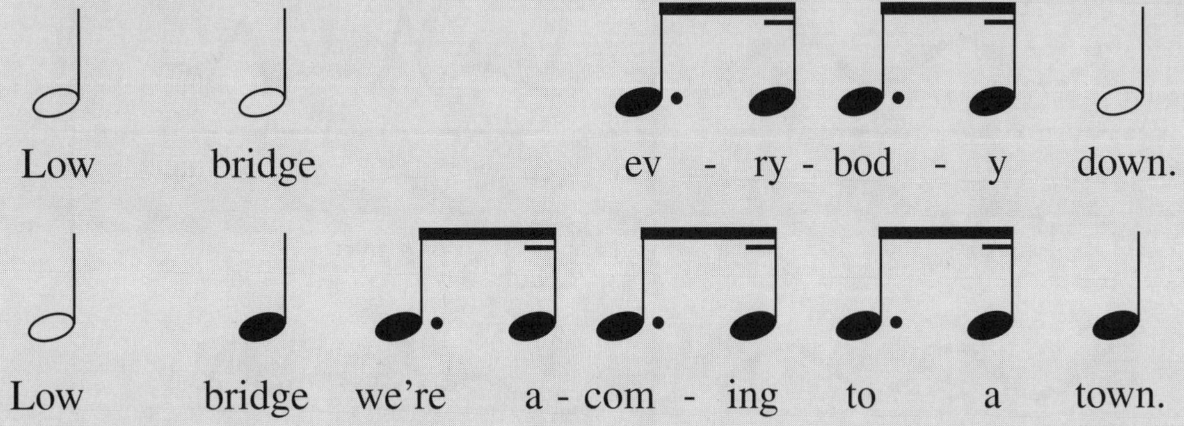

The Erie Canal

Even or Uneven

Directions: Listen for even or uneven eighth notes, and mark your answer with an X in the box.

1.	☐ even	☐ uneven
2.	☐ even	☐ uneven
3.	☐ even	☐ uneven
4.	☐ even	☐ uneven
5.	☐ even	☐ uneven

The Erie Canal

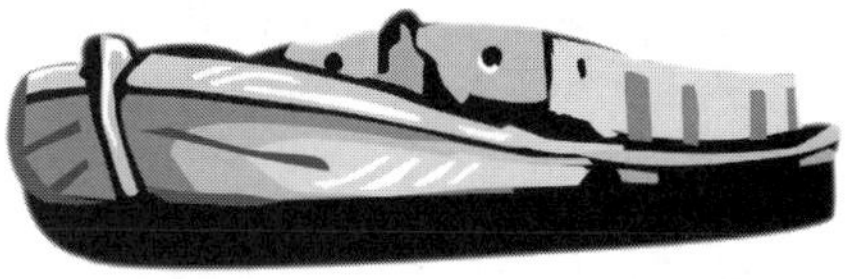

Similar and Different

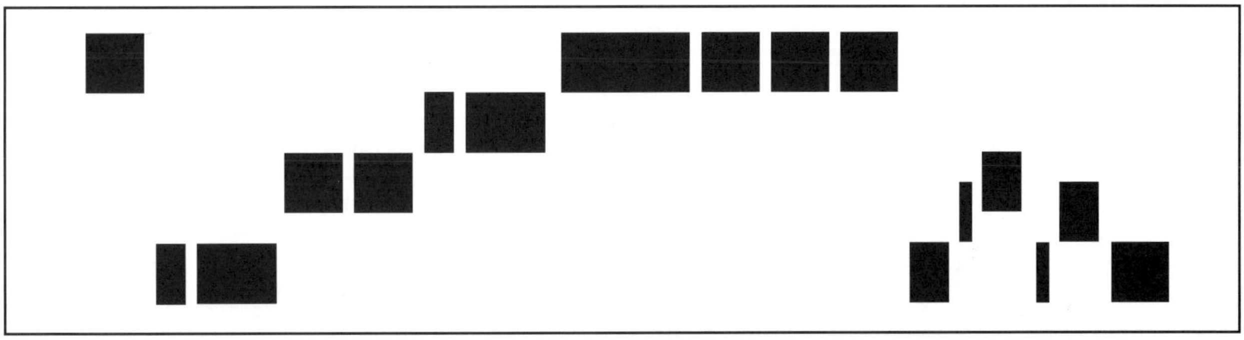

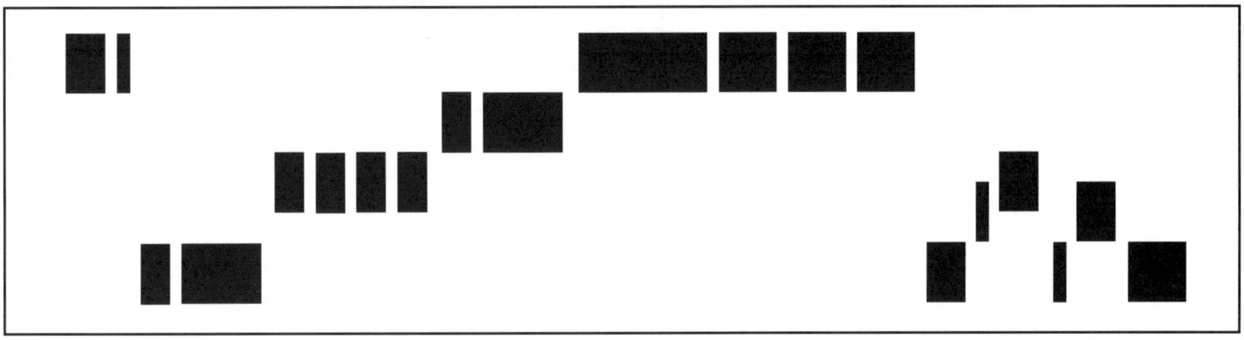

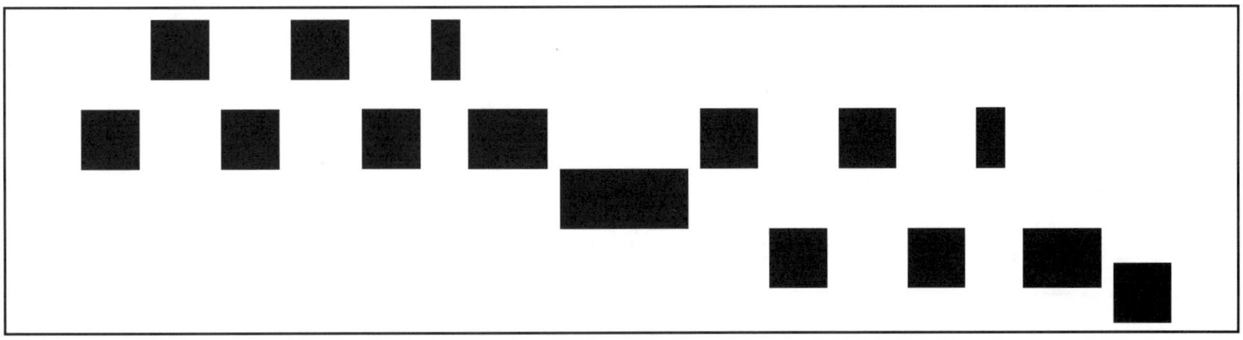

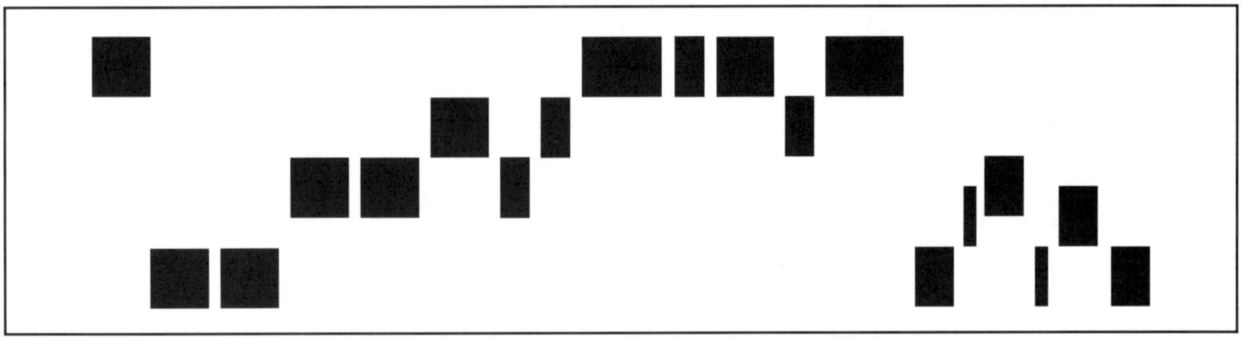

The Erie Canal

Create Your Own AABA

Directions: Create an AABA melody. Use these pitches on bells or keyboard:

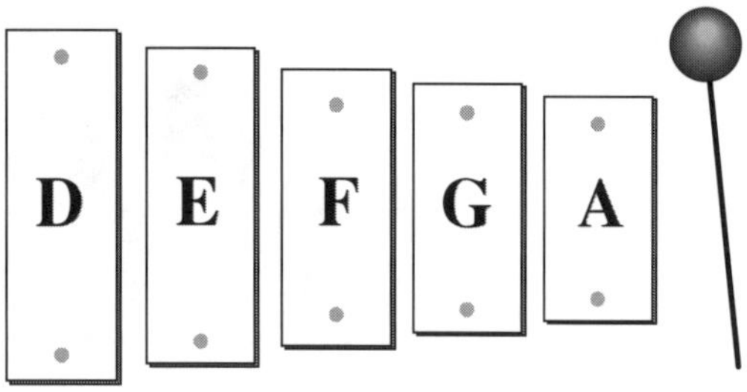

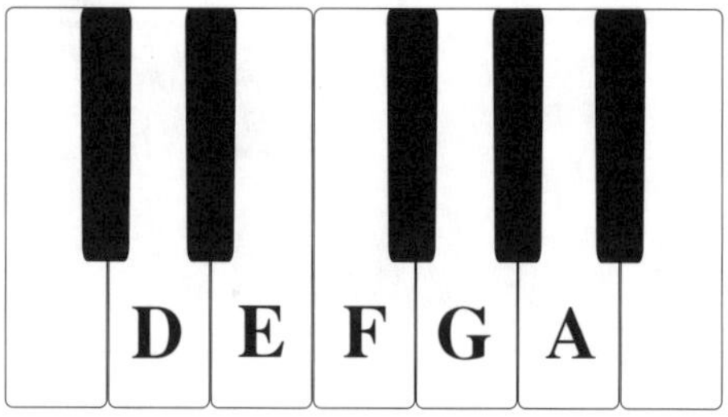

Create an A Pattern:

Create a B Pattern: (Make it sound different from A)

Combine them to create a composition in **AABA** form.

Teacher Instructions

Follow the Drinkin' Gourd

Activity 4-1: Learning about Spirituals

Grade Level: 4-8
National Standard: 1

Objective
Students understand the origin and background of a song.

Materials
- Get America Singing...AGAIN! Volume 2, Singer's Edition, p. 16
- Student copies of 4-1

Directions
Open the class period by singing the song. Ask, "How many of you have heard this song before?" Facilitate a class discussion including any of the following:
- Where students have heard this tune
- What lyrics they recall
- What meaning they attach to the song

Distribute student copies of 4-1. Invite students to read individually in partners, or as a class as appropriate to students' reading abilities. Instruct students to discuss the questions in small groups and then share their responses with the class.

Activity 4-2: Secret Code

Grade Level: 4-8
National Standard: 1

Objective
Students understand the origin and background of a song.

Materials
- Get America Singing...AGAIN! Volume 2, Singer's Edition, p. 16
- Transparency or student copies of 4-2

Directions
Distribute student copies of 4-2. Invite students to read individually, in partners, or as a class as appropriate to students' reading abilities. Use 4-2 as the basis for a class discussion around this topic. Instruct students to work individually as they respond to the journaling questions. Sing "Follow the Drinkin' Gourd" and help students discover additional secret code words and phrases.

Activity 4-3: The Underground Railroad

Grade Level: 4-8
National Standards: 1, 8

Objective
Students understand the origin and background of a song.

Materials
- Get America Singing...AGAIN! Volume 2, Singer's Edition, p. 16
- Transparency or student copies of 4-3
- Research materials or internet access

Directions
Distribute student copies of 4-3. Invite students to read individually, in partners, or as a class as appropriate to students' reading abilities. Invite students to work individually, in partners, or in small groups as they respond to the research questions. Teacher may wish to share with students the book, *Follow the Drinkin' Gourd*, by Jeanette Winter.

Answer Key (Student Responses may include:)

1. *Conductors were free individuals who traveled to the South to guide and/or transport slaves to freedom. Stations were houses or locations where escaping slaves could find food, shelter, and a place to rest before the next leg of the journey.*
2. *Harriet Tubman was one of the most famous "conductors" of the Underground Railroad. She helped several hundred slaves to freedom.*
3. *Answers will vary. Peg Leg Joe is said to have been a free African American who traveled from plantation to plantation, teaching slaves the routes to freedom.*

Activity 4-4: Bell and Keyboard Harmony

Grade Level: 3-6
National Standard: 2

Objective
Students play chords to accompany a song.

Materials
- Get America Singing...AGAIN! Volume 2, Singer's Edition, p. 16
- Transparency of 4-4
- Bells and mallets; keyboards

Directions
Display a transparency of 4-4. Help students learn to play the E minor and B minor triads as represented on the page. Select students to play the chords on measures 9-10 and measures 17-18, as the class sings.

Activity 4-5: Researching Spirituals

Grade Level: 4-8
National Standard: 9

Objective
Students understand the origin and background of a song.

Materials
- Get America Singing…AGAIN! Volume 2, Singer's Edition, p. 16
- Student copies of 4-5
- Pencils
- Research materials or internet access

Directions
Distribute student copies of 4-5. Instruct students to cut the cards apart, and then work individually, in partners, or in small to find information about spirituals. Encourage students to share their research.

Activity 4-6: Show What You Know

Grade Level: 5-8
National Standards: 1, 9

Objective
Students understand the origin and background of songs in their varied repertoire.

Materials
- Get America Singing…AGAIN! Volume 2, Singer's Edition, p. 16
- Student copies of 4-6
- Pencils

Directions
Distribute student copies of 4-6. Instruct students to work individually, in partners, or in small groups. Debrief the activity by encouraging students to share their responses with the class.

Follow the Drinkin' Gourd

Learning about Spirituals

From the days of slavery in the United States (the late1600s through the mid-1800s), African Americans created and sang spirituals. These songs very often expressed the sorrow of a life of oppression forced upon slaves by plantation owners and masters.

It was common for an African-American spiritual to have more than one verse, have lyrics which repeated from verse to verse, and to have a refrain. The lyrics, often based on stories from the Bible, allowed slaves to share their religious beliefs with one another. At camp meetings, African-American men, women, and children would listen to preachers, sing spirituals, and dance for many hours.

Lyrics of spirituals often spoke of freedom, the promised land, and a better life. Some spirituals carried a secret code. Slaves used the code to send messages about escaping to the North.

Questions for Discussion

1. What are the titles of some spirituals that you already know or have heard?

2. What do you recall about the songs, the lyrics, or the messages they contained?

3. How important were spirituals to African-American slaves?

Follow the Drinkin' Gourd

Secret Code

Some spirituals carried a secret code. The words held a secret meaning which helped slaves send messages about escape. Because slaves were severely punished if they were ever caught talking about escape, they needed to send messages in a code that owners and masters would not know.

"Follow the Drinkin' Gourd" is one of the best known secret code spirituals. Following are some of the possible messages conveyed by the lyrics:

When the sun comes back and the first quail calls
This time of year may have been best to begin the escape. Quails migrated into the South for the winter. For some slaves, the journey to freedom took well up to a year or more. If a slave escaped "when the sun came back and the first quail called," he or she would possibly arrive at the Ohio River about a year later, when it was frozen again, and would be able to walk across the ice.

The drinkin' gourd
The "drinkin' gourd" was the Big Dipper which points directly to the North Star (also called "Polaris"). Slaves were taught to identify Polaris using the Big Dipper, so that they could use the star to guide their journey in the right direction - toward the North where they would be free.

The old man
The "old man" may have been a reference to someone who would guide them north to freedom. The Old Man may have been "Peg Leg Joe," who was said to have traveled throughout the South, passing along escape instructions to African Americans.

Questions for Journaling

1. What do you already know about slavery and slaves' escapes to freedom?
2. If you had been an African-American slave, what might you have considered before you decided whether to attempt an escape following the Drinkin' Gourd?

Follow the Drinkin' Gourd

The Underground Railroad

Even though plantation owners believed that their slaves knew little or nothing about geography, quite the opposite was true. One thing slaves knew was that freedom was North, and the North Star, or Polaris, pointed the way to that freedom. But, even with a star to guide them, slaves knew that they faced a very dangerous and risky journey.

Through the Underground Railroad, slaves received information about routes that would take them to freedom. The Underground Railroad sent messengers to the South to travel from plantation to plantation and teach slaves how to escape.

The Underground Railroad was not underground nor a railroad. It was not made of trains and tracks. Instead, it was a system of paths, rivers, boats, wagons, and safe locations along the way, helping slaves as they made their way to freedom. Using recommended routes, slaves traveled at night. They waded through water to keep dogs from following their scent. Sometimes when it was too risky to travel, they took shelter at safe houses until it was safe again. Some slaves were transported for parts of the journey in wagons or "chariots."

Questions for Research

1. In the Underground Railroad, what was a "station?" What was a "conductor?"

2. Who was Harriet Tubman?

3. What can you find out about "Peg Leg Joe?"

Follow the Drinkin' Gourd

Bell and Keyboard Harmony

Play an E minor triad (E-G-B)

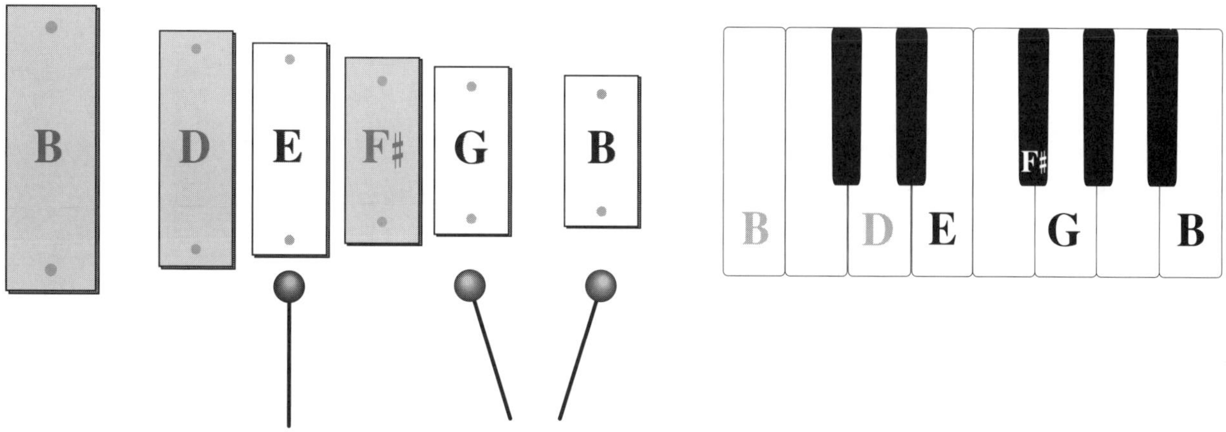

Play a B minor triad (B-D-F#)

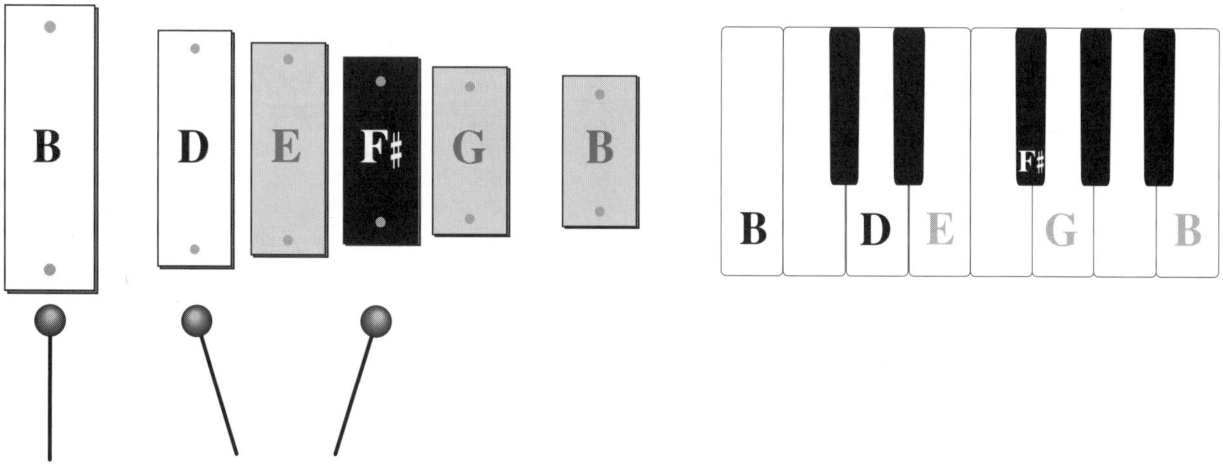

Em Bm Em

Fol - low the drink - in' gourd

Follow the Drinkin' Gourd

Researching Spirituals

Directions: Using interviews, books, music books, the media center, the internet, and any other resources, find as many spirituals as you can. Take notes about each example you find. Compare your information with the information that other students discover.

Title ______________________

Source ______________________

Notes about a religious reference: ______________________

Notes about repeating lyrics: ______________________

Notes about a refrain: ______________________

Any text that might contain a hidden (escape) message: ______________________

____

Title ______________________

Source ______________________

Notes about a religious reference: ______________________

Notes about repeating lyrics: ______________________

Notes about a refrain: ______________________

Any text that might contain a hidden (escape) message: ______________________

____

Title ______________________

Source ______________________

Notes about a religious reference: ______________________

Notes about repeating lyrics: ______________________

Notes about a refrain: ______________________

Any text that might contain a hidden (escape) message: ______________________

____

Title ______________________

Source ______________________

Notes about a religious reference: ______________________

Notes about repeating lyrics: ______________________

Notes about a refrain: ______________________

Any text that might contain a hidden (escape) message: ______________________

____

Follow the Drinkin' Gourd

Show What You Know

Name______________________________ Class__________ Date________

Write your answers to the following questions:

1. Write something interesting that you learned about African-American spirituals.

____
____
____
____
____
____
____

2. Decode the secret messages communicated in the lyrics of the song "Follow the Drinkin' Gourd."

____
____
____
____
____
____
____

3. Write a paragraph about the Underground Railroad and the ways that it helped slaves escape to freedom.

____
____
____
____
____
____
____

Teacher Instructions

I Got Rhythm

Activity 5-1, 5-2: About the Composer, A Gershwin Puzzler

Grade Level: 5-8
National Standard: 1

Objective
Students understand the origin and background of a song.

Materials
- Get America Singing…AGAIN! Volume 2, Singer's Edition, p. 22
- Student copies of 5-1 and 5-2
- Pencils
- Research materials or internet access

Directions
Distribute student copies of 5-1. About the Composer. Invite students to read individually or as a class as appropriate to students' reading abilities. Distribute copies of 5-2. Instruct students to work individually, in partners, or in small groups to find answers to the puzzle questions. Encourage students to share their responses as well as other interesting information about Gershwin.

Answer Key:
ACROSS 1. Pan 2. Brooklyn 3. Rhapsody 5. Sing 7. American 9. Me
DOWN 1. Porgy 2. Swanee 3. Ira 8. Rhythm

Activity 5-3: Getting Rhythm

Grade Level: 5-8
National Standard: 6

Objective
Students listen and identify elements of rhythm.

Materials
- Get America Singing…AGAIN! Volume 2, Singer's Edition, p. 22
- Student copies of 5-3

Directions
Choose one phrase from a simple children's rhyme such as "Twinkle Twinkle Little Star." Clap and chant the rhyme, changing elements of rhythm. For example:

1. Perform with a triple meter, e.g.,

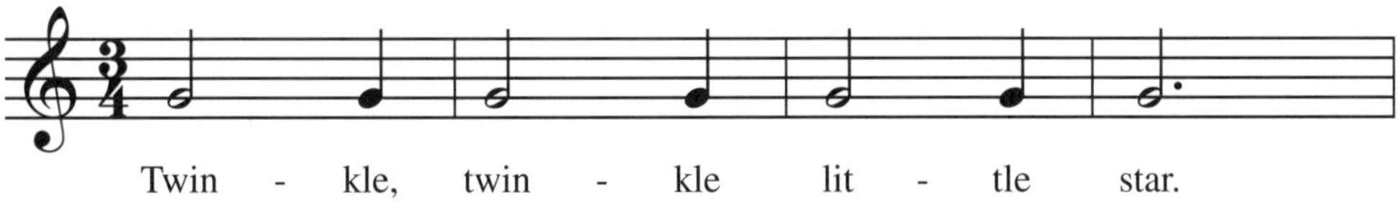

2. Perform with a nebulous and/or unsteady beat.
3. Perform with a faster or slower tempo.
4. Change the melodic rhythm, e.g.,

Invite students to identify the rhythmic element that is changed each time, and mark their student pages.

Repeat the exercise using one phrase from the song "I Got Rhythm."

Activity 5-4: Body Percussion

Grade Level: 3-6
National Standard: 5

Objective
Students read and perform using body percussion.

Materials
- Get America Singing…AGAIN! Volume 2, Singer's Edition, p. 22
- Transparency or student copies of 5-4

Directions
Display the transparency or distribute student copies of 5-4. Assuming prior experience with rhythm reading, rehearse each part, and layer percussion assignments throughout the class. (Note stems up and stems down to indicate left and right.) Select a student conductor to lead the performance. Perform with the song "I Got Rhythm."

Activity 5-5: Elements of Music

Grade Level: 4-8
National Standard: 6

Objective
Students create a visual representation for each of the elements of music.

Materials
- Get America Singing…AGAIN! Volume 2, Singer's Edition, p. 22
- Transparency and student copies of 5-5
- Pencils

Directions
Begin the class with a review of elements of music. Introduce the term "metaphor" and provide several examples. e.g., "Rhythm is like the sound of footsteps in the hallways – because we hear short, long, even, and uneven patterns;" "Melody is like a roller coaster, because it goes up, goes down, and sometimes stays the same." Divide students into small groups and distribute one copy of 5-5 to each group. Instruct students to follow page directions and create a visual representation and written explanation for each element of music. Invite groups to share their work with the class.

Activity 5-6: A Rhythm Complex

Grade Level: 2-4
National Standards: 2, 5

Objective
Students read icons and perform a rhythm complex.

Materials
- Get America Singing…AGAIN! Volume 2, Singer's Edition, p. 22
- Transparency and student copies of 5-6

Directions
Display transparency of 5-6. As a class, clap and chant each line of the rhythm complex. To demonstrate, select students to play each instrument. Begin with the drum part. As the drum player repeats his/her pattern, "layer" additional parts. Instruct each part to continue to repeat until entire complex is performing together. Divide class into groups of four. Instruct students to rehearse and perform their own rhythm complexes modeled after the class demonstration. (NOTE: blank space = silence.)

Activity 5-7: Create a Rhythm Complex

Grade Level: 2-4
National Standards: 2, 4, 5

Objective

Students create and perform their own rhythm complex.

Materials

- Get America Singing...AGAIN! Volume 2, Singer's Edition, p. 22
- Transparency and student copies of 5-7

Directions

Display transparency of 5-7. Invite students to create patterns for each instrument, using the suggested durations on the page. Fill in the patterns and perform the complex as a class demonstration. Divide class into groups of four. Instruct students to follow directions as printed, and create their own rhythm complexes modeled after the class demonstration.

Activity 5-8: Syncopation

Grade Level: 4-8
National Standard: 5

Objective

Students read and perform patterns with and without syncopation.

Materials

- Get America Singing...AGAIN! Volume 2, Singer's Edition, p. 22
- Transparency of 5-8

Directions

Display transparency of 5-8. Guide students to follow the directions on the page, clapping and chanting rhythm syllables (or numeric counts) for rhythm patterns. Guide students to formulate their own definition of the term "syncopation." As a class, look up the term in a dictionary or glossary and compare.

Answer Key (Student Responses may include:)
Syncopation – a shift, placing emphasis on an unaccented beat

I Got Rhythm

About the Composer

Jacob Gershovitz was born in Brooklyn, New York, in 1898, just two years before the twentieth century began. He later changed his name to George Gershwin.

As a young boy, growing up in Manhattan, he was an active youngster, loving the outdoors and especially roller skating. His parents bought a piano for his older brother, Ira, but George convinced them that he should get to take the piano lessons instead. Later in life he would come to write the music and his brother would write the words, as the two of them worked together on many songs.

George worked for a music company, demonstrating songs to customers, but soon decided that he wanted to compose his own songs. George's first hit, "Swanee," was published when he was only nineteen years old. It was recorded onto one of the very first phonograph records ever made and became very popular with the American public.

Throughout his life, George continued to compose popular songs and musicals. His opera "Porgy and Bess," featured songs such as "Summertime," and "I Got Plenty o' Nuthin'." He also composed musical scores for several Hollywood films and is well known for his very famous orchestral piece, "Rhapsody in Blue."

He died at the young age of 38, of a brain tumor.

George Gershwin is remembered for bridging a gap between popular music and concert music, and adding a jazz influence to classical music. His music was widely respected by fellow musicians and music lovers of all ages.

I Got Rhythm

A Gershwin Puzzler

Across

1. Tin ________ Alley
2. George's birthplace
3. "_______ in Blue"
5. "Of Thee I ______"
7. "An _______ in Paris"
9. "Somebody Loves ___"

Down

1. "________ and Bess"
4. Gershwin's first hit song
6. George's brother
8. "I Got _______"

I Got Rhythm

Getting Rhythm

Defining terms

Steady Beat	*the underlying pulse*
Melodic Rhythm	*organization of shorter and longer sounds over a steady pulse*
Meter	*organization of beats into patterns, often 2s or 3s*
Tempo	*speed*

1. ☐ steady beat ☐ meter
   ☐ melodic rhythm ☐ tempo

2. ☐ steady beat ☐ meter
   ☐ melodic rhythm ☐ tempo

3. ☐ steady beat ☐ meter
   ☐ melodic rhythm ☐ tempo

4. ☐ steady beat ☐ meter
   ☐ melodic rhythm ☐ tempo

5. ☐ steady beat ☐ meter
   ☐ melodic rhythm ☐ tempo

6. ☐ steady beat ☐ meter
   ☐ melodic rhythm ☐ tempo

I Got Rhythm

Body Percussion

By Loretta Norgon

I Got Rhythm

Elements of Music

Melody is like

because ______________________

____

Rhythm is like

because ______________________

____

Harmony is like

because ______________________

____

Form is like

because ______________________

____

Timbre is like

because ______________________

____

I Got Rhythm

A Rhythm Complex

Directions: With your group, choose an instrument and a player for each layer of this complex. Practice your complex. Perform it for your class.

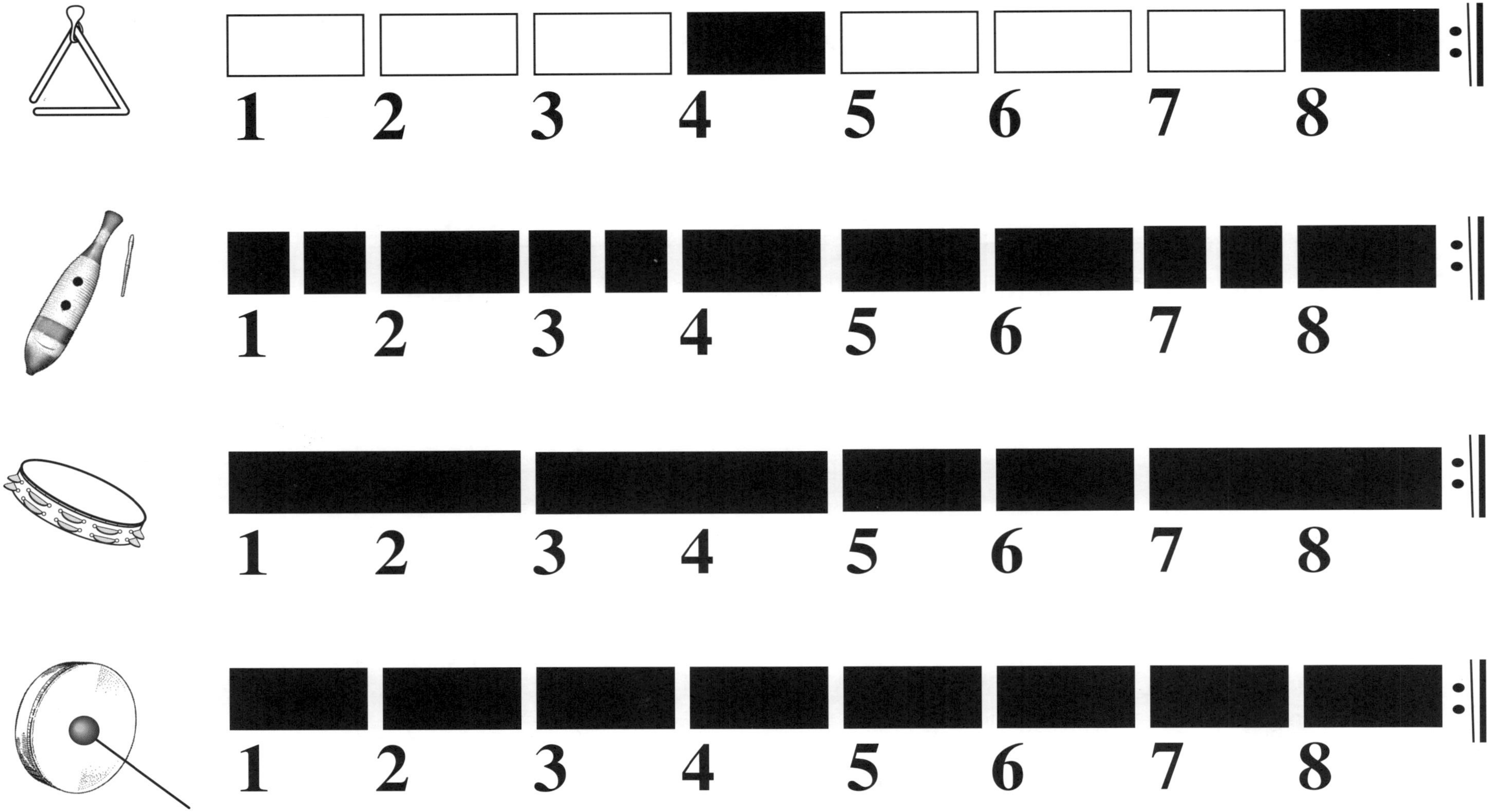

I Got Rhythm

Create a Rhythm Complex

Directions: With your group, create a rhythm pattern for each instrument. Fill in the spaces below to show your patterns. For silent beats, leave spaces blank. Practice your complex. Perform it for your class.

You may use 2 short sounds · one sound that matches the beat · one longer sound, as long as two beats

1	2	3	4	5	6	7	8

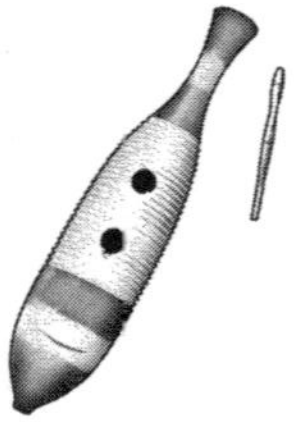

1	2	3	4	5	6	7	8

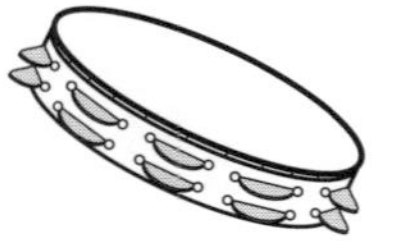

1	2	3	4	5	6	7	8

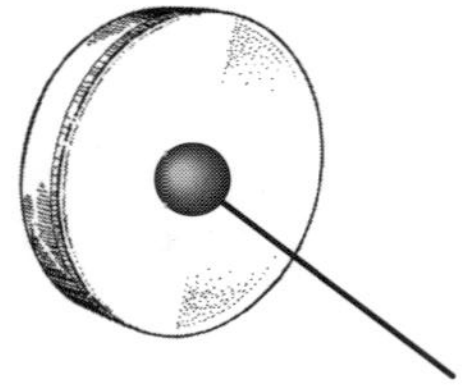

Foundation - the steady beat

1	2	3	4	5	6	7	8

I Got Rhythm

Syncopation

1. Clap and chant. Find the strong beats.

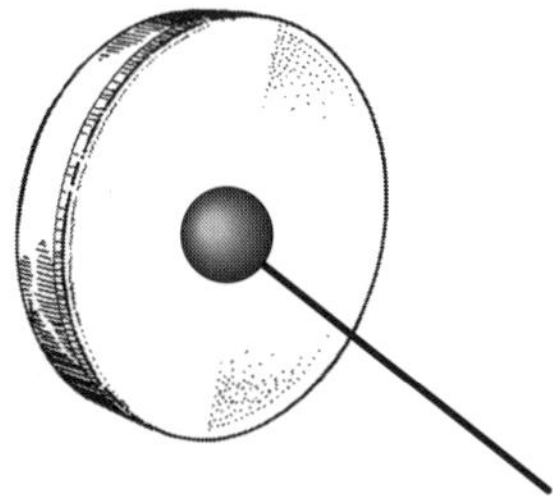

2. Clap and chant. Find the strong beats.

Syncopation

turns a weak beat into a strong beat

3. Clap and chant these examples. Check the ones that use syncopation

☐ 

☐ 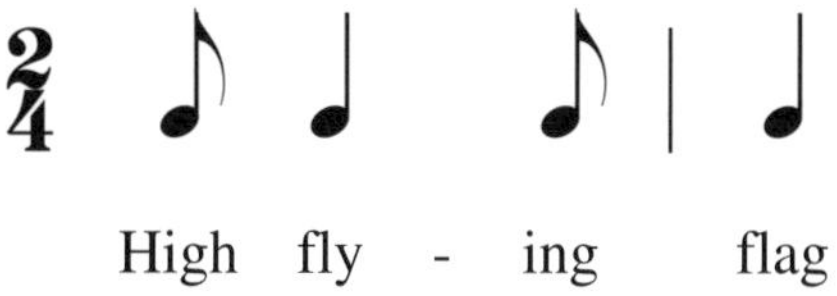

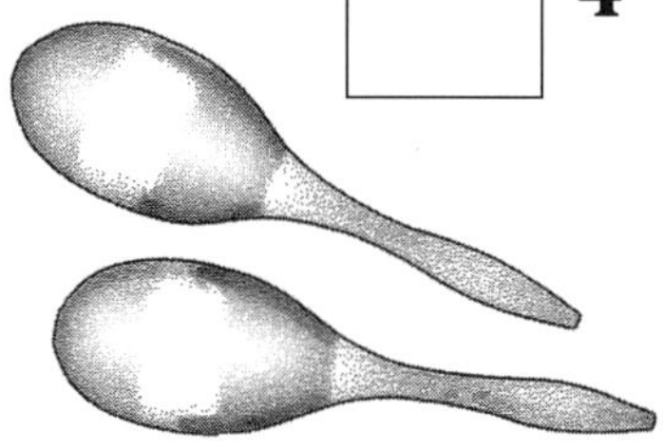

☐ 

☐ 

4. Find syncopation in "I Got Rhythm."

Old MacDonald Had a Farm

Activity 6-1: Make a Map

Grade Level: K-1
National Standard: 1

Objective
Students sing a song from memory.

Materials
- Get America Singing...AGAIN! Volume 2, Singer's Edition, p. 32
- Transparency and student copies of 6-1
- Scissors
- Envelopes for each student

Directions
Display transparency of 6-1. Help students use the illustrations as they learn the lyrics and melody of the song. Distribute student copies. Assist students as they cut out the cards and sequence them to create their own song maps and sing the song. Distribute an envelope for each student. Encourage students to take their cards home and perform the song for their families.

Activity 6-2: Read and Sing

Grade Level: 1-2
National Standards: 1, 5, 6

Objective
Students follow icons, sing, and discover the form of a song.

Materials
- Get America Singing...AGAIN! Volume 2, Singer's Edition, p. 32
- Transparency and student copies of 6-2

Directions
Display transparency. Help students follow the icons to sing each phrase. As a class, analyze and discuss the similarities and differences in each phrase. Help class discover that phrases 1, 2, and 4 are similar and that phrase 3 is different, (i.e. basic AABA form.) Distribute student copies. Help students follow the icons as they sing the song again. Encourage them to take their maps home to perform the song for members of their families.

Activity 6-3: Play Along

Grade Level: 1-2
National Standard: 2

Objective
Students perform easy melodic patterns on bells.

Materials
- Get America Singing…AGAIN! Singer's Edition, p. 32
- Transparency and Student copies of 6-3
- Resonator bells B, A, G and mallets

Directions
Display the transparency or distribute student copies of 6-3. Help students read the icons and match them to the melody. Select individual students to play the melody fragment. Sing the song with the class. Invite individuals to play along. Perform the entire song. Select other students to play as the class sings.

Activity 6-4: Find the Patterns

Grade Level: 3-4
National Standard: 5

Objective
Students identify notated rhythm patterns.

Materials
- Get America Singing…AGAIN! Volume 2, Singer's Edition, p. 32
- Student copies of 6-4
- Wood block or other classroom rhythm instrument
- Pencils

Directions
Begin the class with a review of eighth and quarter notes. Distribute student copies of 6-4. Play one of the examples in #1. Instruct students to show which pattern they hear by marking an "X" in the appropriate space. Continue with additional examples.

Activity 6-5: Name That Tune

Grade Level: K-2
National Standard: 6

Objective
Students identify melodies of familiar songs.

Materials
- Get America Singing...AGAIN! Volume 2, Singer's Edition, p. 32
- Transparency and student copies of 6-5
- Plastic counting chips
- (Optional) keyboard or other melodic instrument

Directions
Distribute student copies of 6-5 and one counting chip for each student. Invite students to listen to one phrase from a familiar song (performed by teacher on piano, recorder, or neutral syllable with singing voice). Suggest that students listen to the melody, and place a chip on one space to show which song they heard. Continue with other examples on the page, ending with "Old Mac Donald Had a Farm."

Activity 6-6, 6-7: Ideas for New Lyrics, New Lyrics

Grade Level: 2-3
National Standard: 4

Objective
Students create new verses for a familiar song.

Materials
- Get America Singing...AGAIN! Volume 2, Singer's Edition, p. 32
- Transparency and student copies of 6-6, 6-7
- Pencils

Directions
Sing "Old Mac Donald Had a Farm." To class: "What if this song was not about farm animals? How could we sing the song about someone or something else? Let's make up our own words." (See sample below.) Display transparency of 6-6. Invite class to contribute ideas for a new verse for the song, record ideas (words or pictures) in the spaces. Display transparency of 6-7, and fill in the spaces to finish the verse. Distribute student copies of 6-6 and 6-7 and pencils. As individuals, partners, or small groups, invite students to start with the "idea page" and then create and sing their own verses. Encourage students to share their verses with the class.

Sample Idea

Mr. Jackson had a band, E-I-E-I-O.
And in his band he had a drum, E-I-E-I-O.
With a tap-tap here, and a tap-tap there.
Here a tap, there a tap, everywhere a tap-tap.
Mr. Jackson had a band, E-I-E-I-O.

Activity 6-8: Describe and Improvise

Grade Level: K-2
National Standards: 3, 6

Objective

Students describe sounds with graphics and movement, and improvise with instruments.

Materials

- Get America Singing...AGAIN! Volume 2, Singer's Edition, p. 32
- 2 Copies of Transparency of 6-8

Directions

Distribute student copies of 6-8.

Part 1: Display one transparency of 6-8. Invite students to suggest a graphic to illustrate the sound of "quack-quack." Select one student to show his/her idea with movement. A possible student response is two "starbursts" for the graphic. The movement might be hands going from closed fists to open hands twice for the "quack quack." As a class, agree on a graphic to illustrate the sound and movement on the chart. Sing the song, adding the movement. Continue with other verses.

Part 2: Display second copy of 6-8 transparency. Invite students to suggest an instrument (and an idea for how to play it) to substitute for the "quack-quack" sound of the duck. Select one student to play the sound, and, as the class sings, substitute the instrumental improvisation in phrase #3. Add a picture of the instrument (along with another graphic to illustrate the sound idea) and the student's name to the transparency. Continue with other animals, and perform the entire song with instrumental improvisations.

Activity 6-9: Up, Down, Same

Grade Level: K-1
National Standard: 6

Objective
Students identify melodic direction.

Materials
- Get America Singing…AGAIN! Volume 2, Singer's Edition, p. 32
- Transparency and student copies of 6-9
- Plastic counting chips
- Bellset, keyboard, or other melodic instrument

Directions
Begin the class by singing "E-I-E-I-O" as notated in the song, and then as notated alternately on the transparency. Review the concept of melody, as pitches move up, move down, and stay the same. Display the transparency. Play one of the examples on the page, and invite students to help determine which example they heard. Place the plastic chip to mark the correct response. Distribute student copies of 6-9 and chips. Instruct students to listen and show what they hear by placing their chips as directed. Continue with the additional examples, ending with the "correct" E-I-E-I-O pattern. Sing the song to end the class period.

Old MacDonald Had a Farm

Make a Map

Old MacDonald
had a farm

And on this farm
he had a ______

Old MacDonald
had a farm

Old MacDonald Had a Farm

Read and Sing

1.

2.

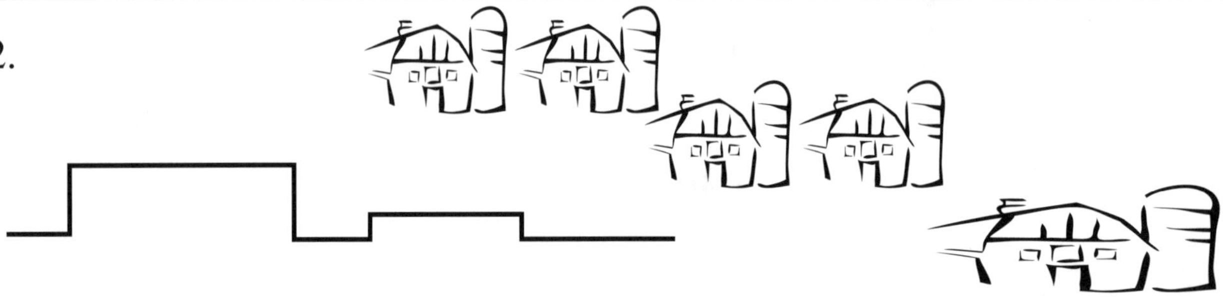

3.

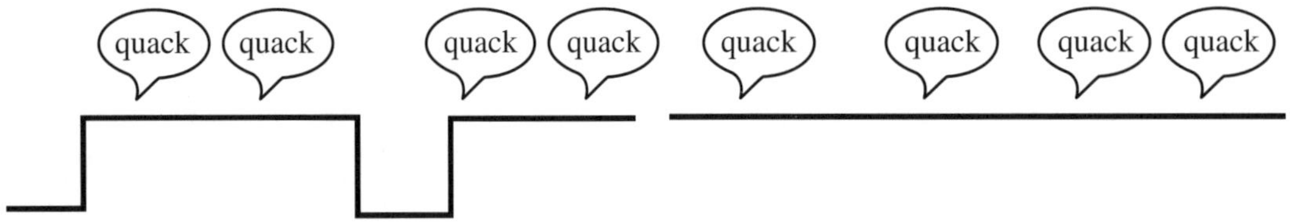

4.

Old MacDonald Had a Farm

Play Along

Directions: Find these bells. Play along with the song.

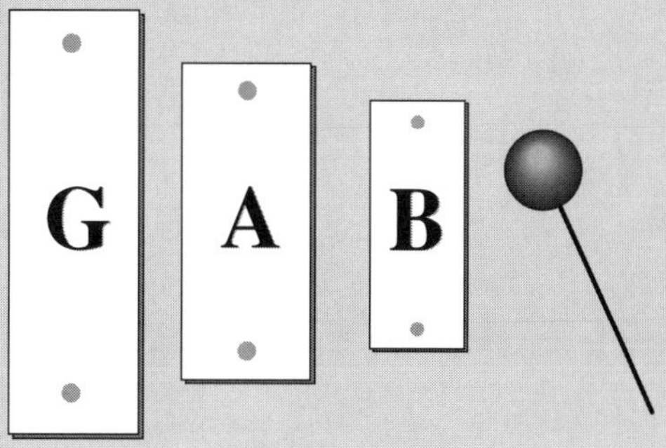

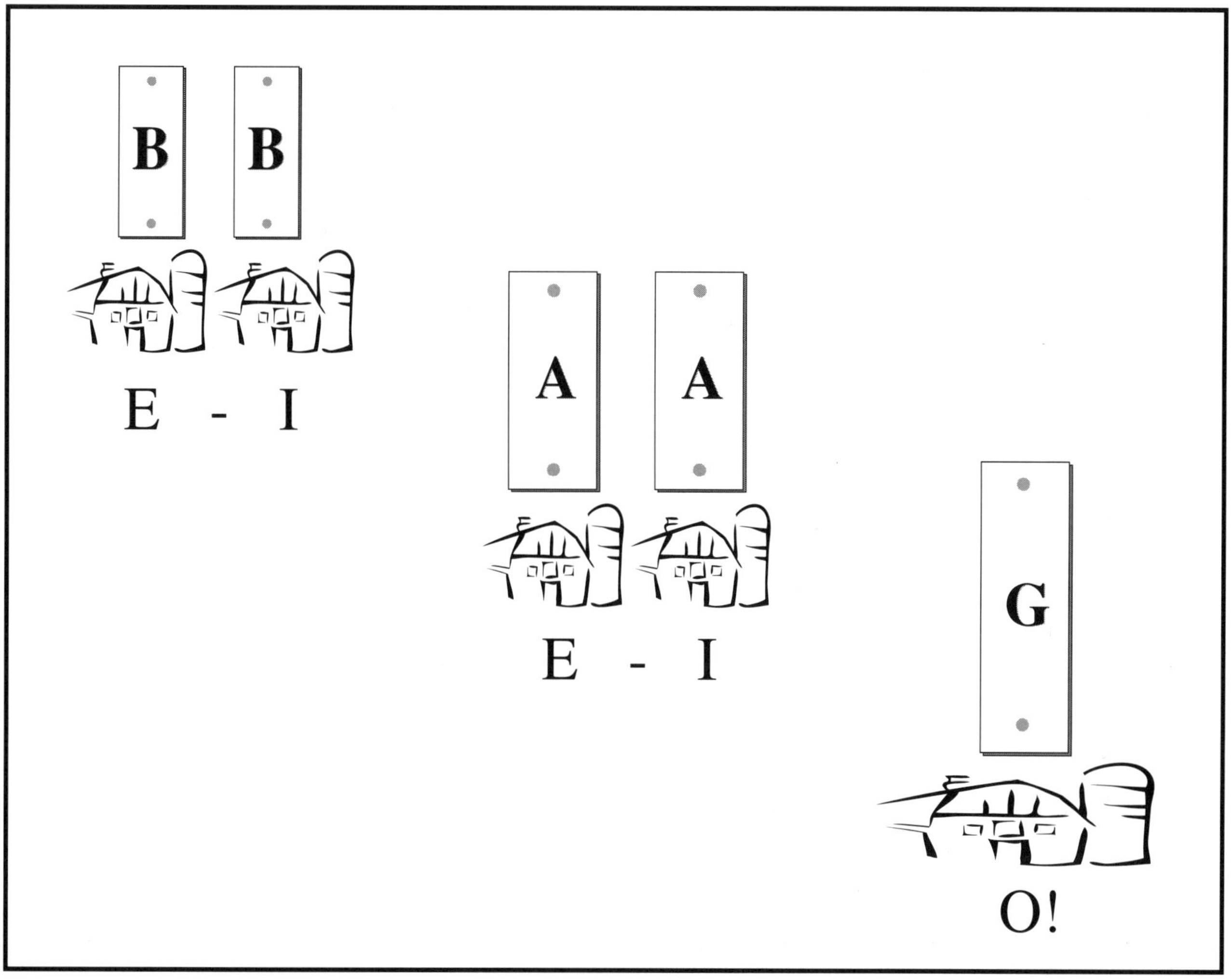

Old MacDonald Had a Farm

Find the Patterns

Directions: Listen to rhythm patterns from the song. Make an X in the box to show the pattern you hear.

1. ☐  ☐ 

2. ☐  ☐ 

3. ☐  ☐ 

4. ☐  ☐ 

5. ☐  ☐ 

Old MacDonald Had a Farm

Name That Tune

Old MacDonald had a farm

Little Peter Rabbit

B-I-N-G-O

Baa Baa Black Sheep

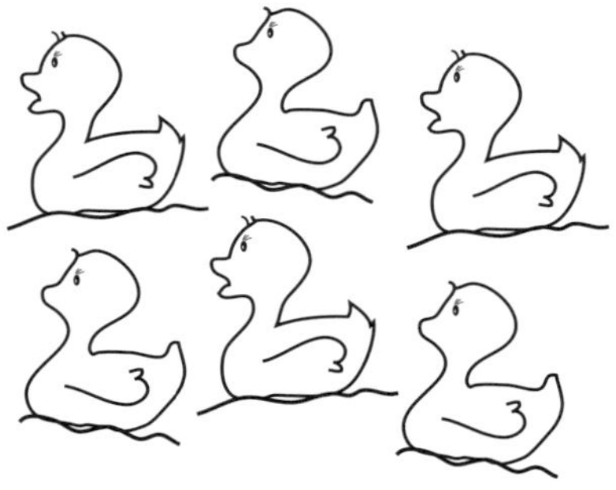

Six Little Ducks

Three Blind Mice

Old MacDonald Had a Farm

Ideas for New Lyrics

Person

Place or group

Parts or members of the group

Sounds

Old MacDonald Had a Farm

New Lyrics

____ had a ____ E-I-E-I-O!

And on his/her ____ he/she had a ____ E-I-E-I-O!

With a ____ here, and a ____ there

Here a ____ there a ____

everywhere a ____

____ had a ____ E-I-E-I-O!

Old MacDonald Had a Farm

Describe and Improvise

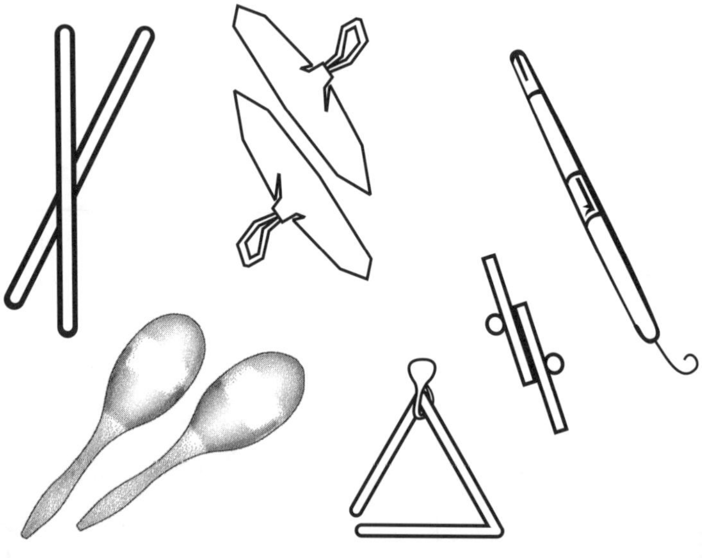

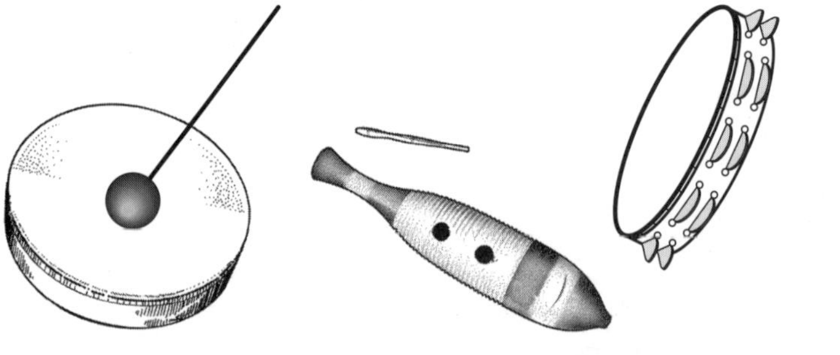

Old MacDonald Had a Farm

Up, Down, Same

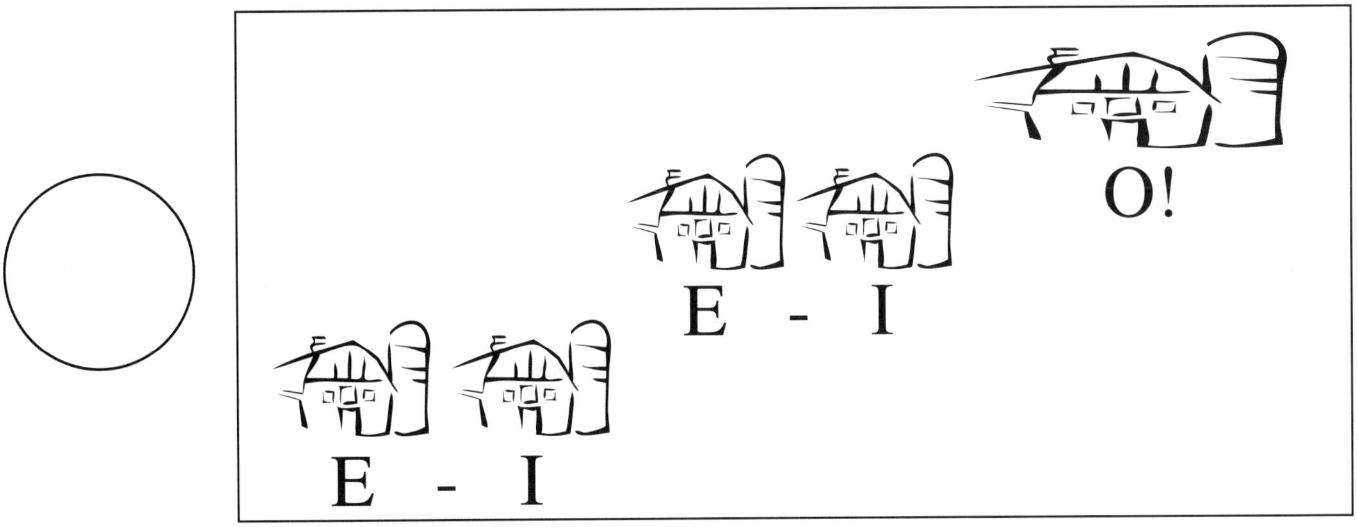

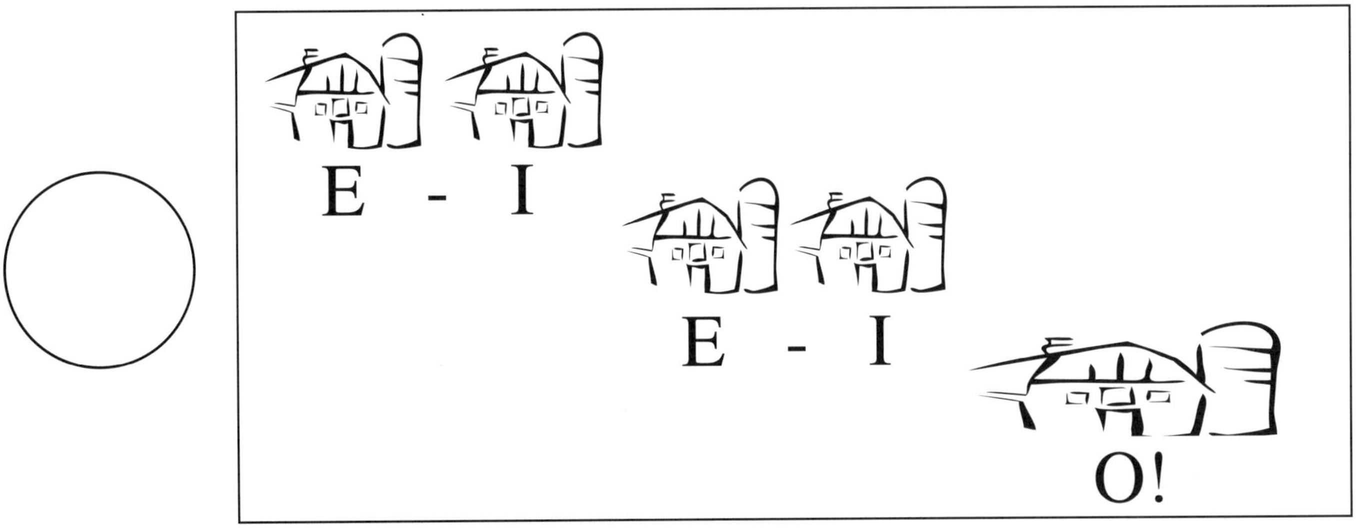

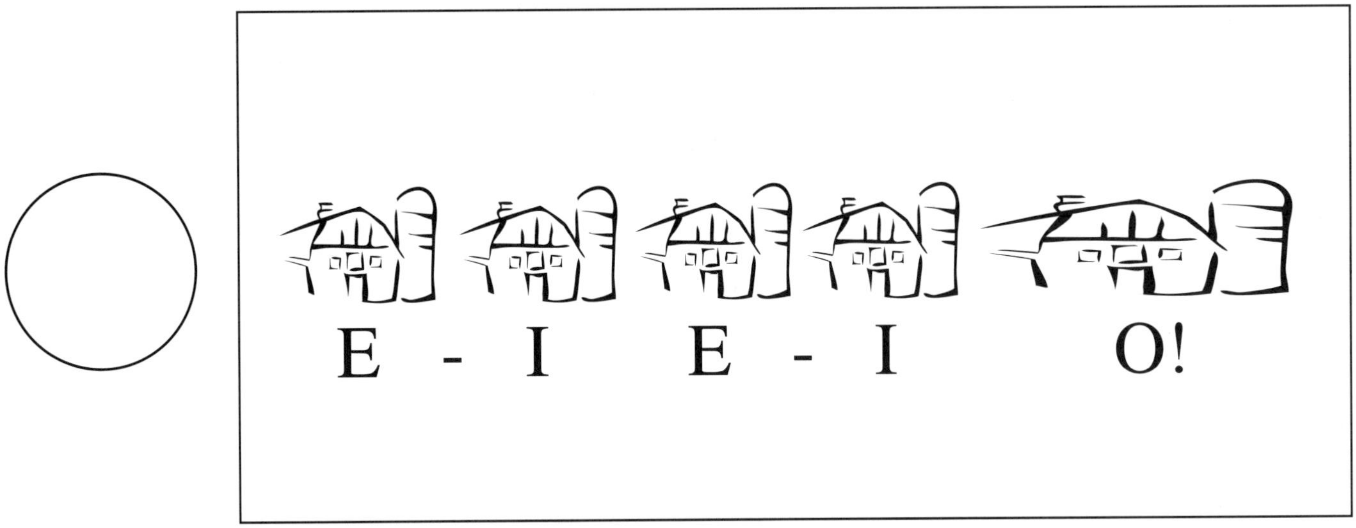

Teacher Instructions

Over the Rainbow

Activity 7-1: Study Guide

Grade Level: 4-6
National Standard: 9

Objective
Students understand the origin and background of a song.

Materials
- Get America Singing…AGAIN! Volume 2, Singer's Edition, p. 33
- Student copies of 7-1
- Pencils
- Research materials or internet access

Directions
Open the class period by singing the song. Ask, "How many of you have seen the movie The Wizard of Oz?" Distribute student copies of 7-1. Invite students to read individually or as a class as appropriate to their reading abilities. Instruct students to work individually, in partners, or in small groups to find answers to the research questions. Encourage students to share their responses with the class.

Answer Key (Student Responses may include:)
1. *Judy Garland – starred as Dorothy Gale*
   Ray Bolger – played the role of the Scarecrow
   L. Frank Baum – wrote The Wizard of Oz (the novel)
   Victor Fleming – director of the movie
   Bert Lahr- played the role of the Cowardly Lion
   Jack Haley – played the role of the Tin Woodman
2. *Answers will vary.*
3. *Members of the Academy of Motion Picture Arts and Sciences nominate individuals and groups for outstanding achievement in all aspects of filmmaking.*
4. *Yip Harburg's other songs include "How Are Things in Glocca Morra?" "It's Only a Paper Moon," Look to the Rainbow," Brother, Can You Spare a Dime?"*
5. *Harold Arlen's other songs include "I've Got the World on a String," "It's Only a Paper Moon," "Stormy Weather," and "Ac-cent-tuate the Positive."*

Activity 7-2: Songs from the Musical

Grade Level: 5-8
National Standard: 9

Objective
Students understand the origin and background of songs in their varied repertoire.

Materials
- Get America Singing…AGAIN! Volume 2, Singer's Edition, p. 33
- Student copies of 7-2
- Pencils
- Recording of The Wizard of Oz soundtrack
- Research materials or internet access

Directions
Distribute student copies of 7-2. As individuals, partners, small groups, or entire class, use 7-2 to launch a research project to study the songs from the musical The Wizard of Oz.

Who sings this song?
Over the Rainbow – sung by Dorothy
If I Only Had a Brain – sung by Scarecrow
If I Only Had a Heart – sung by Tin Woodman
If I Only Had the Nerve – sung by Cowardly Lion
Ding Dong the Witch is Dead – sung by the Munchkins in Munchkinland
We're Off to See the Wizard – sung by Dorothy, Tin Woodman, Scarecrow, and Cowardly Lion
If I Were King of the Forest – sung by Cowardly Lion

Musical Characteristics
Student responses will vary, based on backgrounds in musical analysis.

Activity 7-3: Compose Your Own Rainbow Song for Bells and Keyboard

Grade Level: 3-6
National Standard: 4

Objective
Students compose within specified guidelines.

Materials
- Get America Singing…AGAIN! Volume 2, Singer's Edition, p. 33
- Transparency and student copies of 7-3
- Pencils
- Bells or keyboards

Directions
Display transparency. With the class, model the instructions and procedure for creating a short composition based on the lyrics provided. Distribute student copies, bells or keyboards, and pencils. Working individually, in partners, or in small groups, instruct students to follow directions as printed to create their songs. Allow time for groups to create and practice, and invite them to perform for the teacher or the class.

Activity 7-4: Finding Octaves

Grade Level: 3-5
National Standards: 1, 2 and 5

Objective
Students read, sing and play octaves.

Materials
- Get America Singing…AGAIN! Volume 2, Singer's Edition, p. 33
- Student copies of 7-4
- Pencils
- Dictionaries

Directions
Distribute student copies of 7-4. Invite students to read and work individually, in partners, or in small groups to find definitions. Distribute bellsets or keyboards and allow time for all students to play the octaves as notated. Help students examine the printed music to find examples of octaves in the melody. Provide a vocal model and help students practice singing the octaves accurately and musically.

Answer Key (Student Responses may include:)

1. Definitions:

Octet – a group with eight members
Octopus – a sea animal will eight arms
Octagon – a figure with eight sides
In common: "oct" meaning "eight"

Activity 7-5, 7-6: Rainbow Phrases, Planning Movement

Grade Level: 3-5
National Standard: 6

Objective
Students describe phrase lengths through movement.

Materials
- Get America Singing…AGAIN! Volume 2, Singer's Edition, p. 33
- Transparency and student copies of 7-5, Transparency of 7-6.

Directions
Display transparency for 7-5. As you sing the song, follow the map to show phrase lengths. Distribute student pages. Invite students to follow the phrases with their fingertips as they sing the song again. Invite students to suggest ideas for movement to describe the phrases. Display 7-6. Record student ideas on the transparency. Perform the song again, incorporating student ideas for movement.

Over the Rainbow

Study Guide

The Team of Harburg and Arlen

E.Y. (Yip) Harburg and Harold Arlen collaborated to create the very famous song "Over the Rainbow." Harburg wrote the words and Arlen wrote the music. These two men worked together to compose all of the songs in the film *The Wizard of Oz.*

The Wizard of Oz

With legendary stars such as Judy Garland and Ray Bolger, *The Wizard of Oz* is a classic film originally released in 1939. The plot follows Dorothy and her dog Toto over the rainbow to Munchkinland, and down the Yellow Brick Road, along with the Scarecrow, the Tin Woodman, and the Cowardly Lion. Other classic Harburg and Arlen songs from the film include "We're Off to See the Wizard," "If I Were King of the Forest," and "Ding-Dong! The Witch Is Dead." The film earned two Academy Awards for Best Original Score and Best Song, as well as a special award for Judy Garland, and several other nominations, including Best Picture.

Research Projects

1. Who were the following, and what were their connections to the movie, *The Wizard of Oz*?

Judy Garland	Ray Bolger	L. Frank Baum
Victor Fleming	Bert Lahr	Jack Haley

2. Ask a member of your family what they recall about *The Wizard of Oz.*
3. What does it mean to be "nominated for an Oscar?"
4. What were some other songs for which Yip Harburg wrote the lyrics?
5. What were some other Harold Arlen songs?

Over the Rainbow

Songs from the Musical

Directions: "Over the Rainbow" is one of many well-known songs from the classic musical *The Wizard of Oz*. E.Y. (Yip) Harburg wrote the lyrics and Harold Arlen composed the music. Find out more about other songs from this musical. Do some research and fill in the chart below.

Song Title	Who sings this song?	Musical Characteristics
Over the Rainbow		
If I Only Had a Brain		
If I Only Had a Heart		
If I Only Had the Nerve		
Ding Dong the Witch is Dead		
We're Off to See the Wizard		
If I Were King of the Forest		

Over the Rainbow

Compose Your Own Rainbow Song

Directions: Find these bells or keys on your keyboard. Using short and long sounds for the words, make up a melody. Write your pitches in the spaces below. Practice playing and singing your song. Perform it for your teacher.

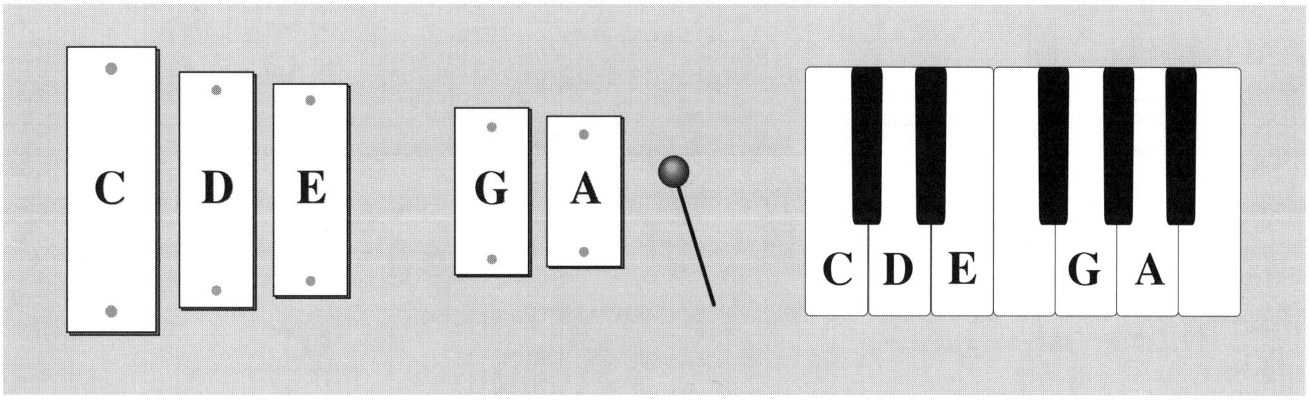

Catch a rain - bow with your eye;

Catch the paint brush in the sky.

Catch a rain - bow, it may seem,

You catch a wish and catch your dream.

Over the Rainbow

Finding Octaves

Look up these words in the dictionary and write their definitions in the blanks:

octet ____

octopus______________________________________

octagon______________________________________

What do all of these words have in common?

The word **octave** is similar to these words also. In an octave, two notes are eight lines or spaces apart. Both notes have the same pitch name. Play these octaves:

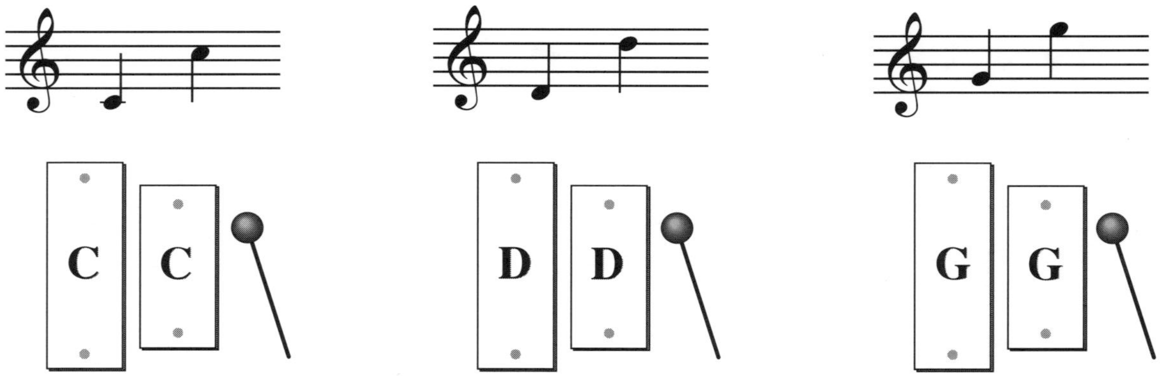

Detective Assignment

Find octaves in the song "Over the Rainbow." Practice singing these intervals so that the octaves are in tune.

Over the Rainbow

Rainbow Phrases

Over the Rainbow

Planning Movement

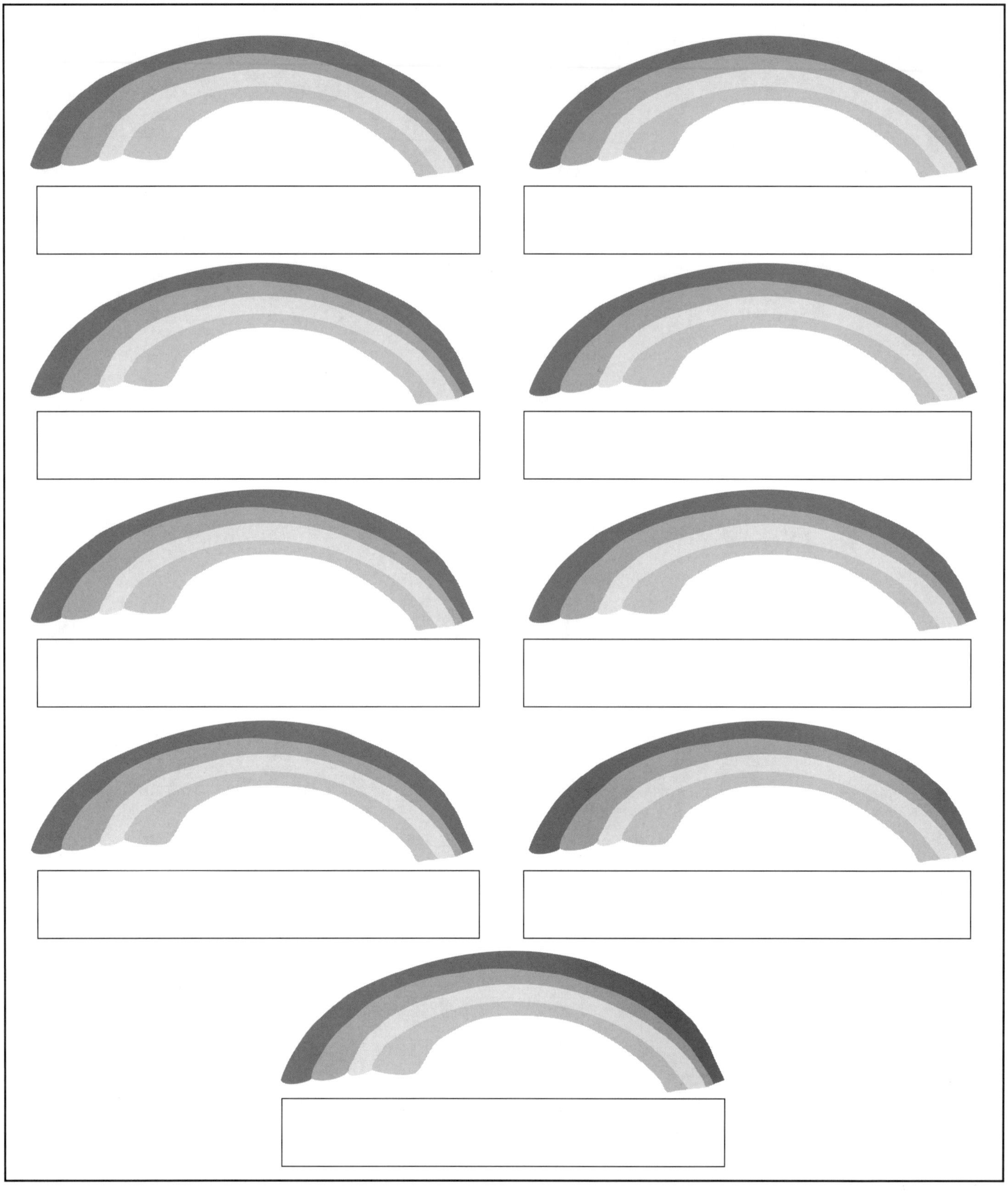

Teacher Instructions

When the Saints Go Marching In

Activity 8-1: Study Guide

Grade Level: 4-6
National Standard: 9

Objective
Students understand the origin and background of a song.

Materials
- Get America Singing...AGAIN! Volume 2, Singer's Edition, p. 48
- Student copies of 8-1
- Pencils
- Research materials or internet access

Directions
Open the class period by singing the song. Ask, "How many of you have heard this song before?" Facilitate a class discussion including any of the following:
- Where students have heard this tune
- What lyrics they recall
- What meaning they attach to the song

Distribute student copies of 8-1. Invite students to read individually or as a class as appropriate to students' reading abilities. Instruct students to work individually, in partners, or in small groups to find answers to the research questions. Encourage students to share their responses with the class.

Answer Key (Student Responses may include:)
1. *Gospel music has roots in spirituals (See 4-1), and in church hymns. Gospel music is characterized by religious themes, high emotion, call and response, choral singing, and soloists who ornament and improvise on the melody line.*
2. *Student answers will vary widely, but may include titles such as "Muskrat Ramble," "Basin Street Blues," or "Way Down Yonder in New Orleans."*
3. *Student answers will vary.*

Activity 8-2: Listening to Dixieland

Grade Level: 5-8
National Standard: 6

Objective
Students identify elements of Dixieland and New Orleans style jazz.

Materials
- Get America Singing...AGAIN! Volume 2, Singer's Edition, p. 48
- Transparency or student copies of 8-2
- Dixieland recording of "When the Saints Go Marching In"

Directions

Display the transparency of 8-2. Using the diagram as a visual reference, facilitate a class discussion about Dixieland and New Orleans style jazz. Share the following information with your students:

Dixieland and the New Orleans style of jazz began in the early 1900s. The groups were small (about 5-8 players) and often times included a trumpet, clarinet, trombone, banjo or guitar, piano, bass and drums. Using popular songs of the time, players would begin by playing all together, all of them improvising at the same time. Next, one by one, the instruments would perform their own improvised solos. Then, the group would play the tune together again, often adding a final section called a tag or coda.

Distribute student copies of 8-2. Listen to the recording and help students identify elements as they occur, and make notes on the page. Compare and discuss what students have noted. If time permits, listen again. Encourage students to read, listen, and research this topic in greater depth.

Activity 8-3: Solfege and Singing with Hand Signs

Grade Level: 2-5
National Standards: 1, 5

Objective

Students read syllables and sing a traditional song.

Materials

- Get America Singing…AGAIN! Volume 2, Singer's Edition, p. 48
- Transparency or student copies of 8-3

Directions

Display the transparency or distribute student copies of 8-3. Assuming prior experience with Solfege and Curwen hand signs, assist students as they read and sing a portion of the song with syllables and signs.

Activity 8-4: Keyboard and Guitar Harmony

Grade Level: 4-8
National Standard: 2

Objective

Students play chords to accompany a song.

Materials
- Get America Singing...AGAIN! Volume 2, Singer's Edition, p. 48
- Transparency 8-4
- Keyboard(s) or Guitar(s)

Directions
Note transposition to G major. Display a transparency of 8-4. Help students learn to play the chords. Select students to play the chords as the class sings the song.

Activity 8-5: Recorder Duet

Grade Level: 3-6
National Standards: 2, 5

Objective
Students read and perform a recorder duet.

Materials
- Get America Singing...AGAIN! Volume 2, Singer's Edition, p. 48
- Student copies of 8-5

Directions
Note transposition to Key of G Major. Distribute student copies of 8-5. Divide class into two groups. Assist one group in learning to play the melody. Assist the other group in learning to play the harmony part. Pair each student with a partner from the opposite group, and allow time for the partners to rehearse their duets. Encourage duets to perform for the class. Reassemble the original groups, and work with each group to help them learn the opposite part. Pair with partners again; allow time for practice, and performances.

Activity 8-6: Adding Orff

Grade Level: 2-4
National Standards: 2, 4, (5)

Objectives
- Students (read and) perform simple instrumental parts while other students sing or play contrasting parts.
- Students create an arrangement.

Materials
- Get America Singing...AGAIN! Volume 2, Singer's Edition, p. 48
- Teacher copy or transparency of 8-6

Directions
Note transposition to Key of G. Teach instrumental parts to students by reading or by rote. With student input, create an arrangement, layering instrumental parts to create a complex and interesting texture.

Activity 8-7: Sequencing Syllables

Grade Level: 2-5
National Standards: 1, 5

Objective
Students read syllables and sequence phrases from a traditional song.

Materials
- Get America Singing…AGAIN! Volume 2, Singer's Edition, p. 48
- Transparency or student copies of 8-7
- Scissors

Directions
Distribute student copies of 8-7 and instruct students to cut the cards apart. Assuming prior experience with solfege, assist students as they read and sing each card, and then sequence them, as they would occur in the song.

Activity 8-8: Partner Songs

Grade Level: 4-8
National Standard: 1

Objective
Students sing partner songs.

Materials
- Get America Singing…AGAIN! Volume 2, Singer's Edition, p. 48
- Student copies of 8-8

Directions
Distribute student copies of 8-8. As students are able to maintain the melody, introduce and rehearse the partner song. Divide the class into two groups. Sing the song with the partner song. Allow groups to reverse parts and sing the songs again.

When the Saints Go Marching In

Study Guide

Getting Started

"When the Saints Go Marching In" is one of the most frequently sung, and best known of American gospel songs. The lyrics were written by American poet, Katherine Davis. A Scottish immigrant, James Black, composed the music. Black also composed another well-known gospel song, "When the Roll is Called Up Yonder."

"When the Saints Go Marching In" was frequently played during New Orleans funeral processions. On the way to the cemetery, the musicians would play very slow and solemn music. On the way back, the mood changed to a celebration, and the musicians would change the mood as they began to improvise on much lighter and happier music. "When the Saints" was one of those celebration songs.

Among the many performances of this song over the years, some of the best known recordings are those by Louis Armstrong (also known as "Satchmo,") and by New Orleans style or Dixieland bands. "Saints" is the most requested song at Preservation Hall, a historic music hall in the French Quarter of New Orleans.

Research Assignment

Find information about the following, and write or type your answers on the back of this page or on a separate page. Be prepared to share and compare your answers with the class.

1. What is gospel music?
2. What are other songs that are frequently played by New Orleans style or Dixieland bands?
3. What can you find out about the funeral procession tradition in New Orleans?

When the Saints Go Marching In

Listening to Dixieland

Directions: Listen to a recording of "When the Saints Go Marching In" played in Dixieland style. As you listen, check the boxes, and write notes to compare what you hear to the items on this chart. As you hear the improvised solos, write a number in each box to show which instrument played first, second, etc. When the recording is over, compare your answers and notes with your class.

1. Introduction ☐

Notes:

2. All instruments together ☐

Notes:

3. Solos ☐

Notes:

☐ Notes:

☐ Notes:

☐ Notes:

☐ Notes:

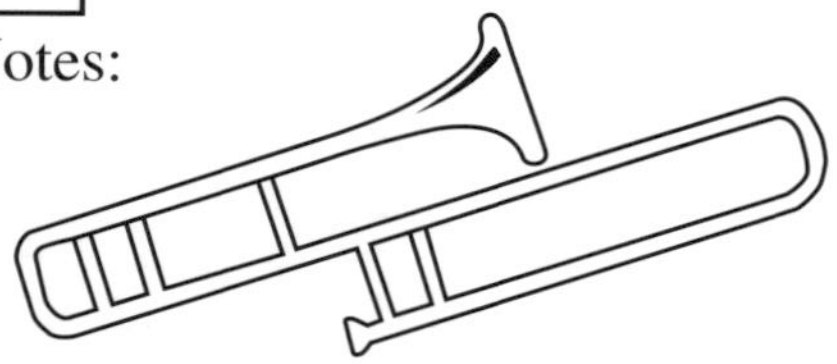

☐ Notes:

☐ Notes:

☐ Notes:

4. All instruments together ☐

Notes:

5. Coda or Tag ☐

Notes:

When the Saints Go Marching In

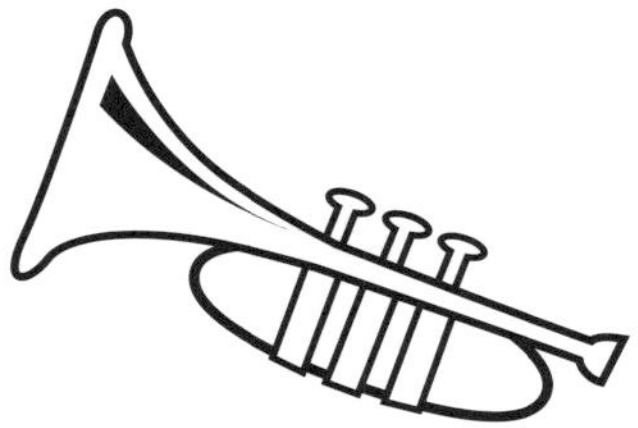

Solfege and Singing With Hand Signs

Directions: Sing the melody using syllables.

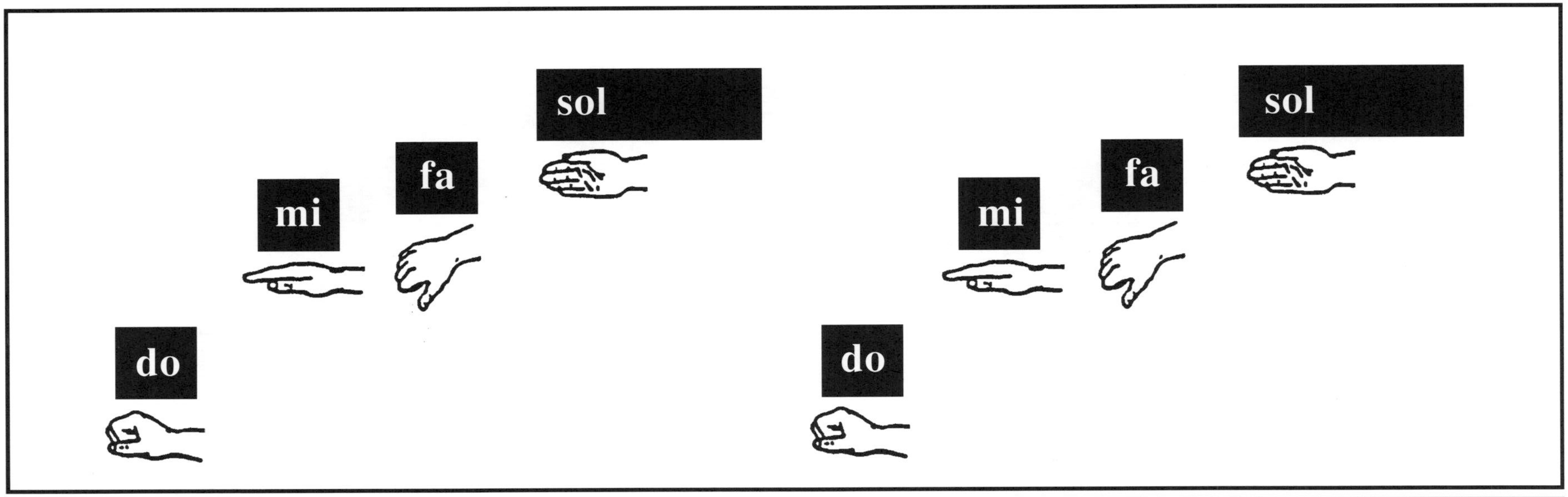

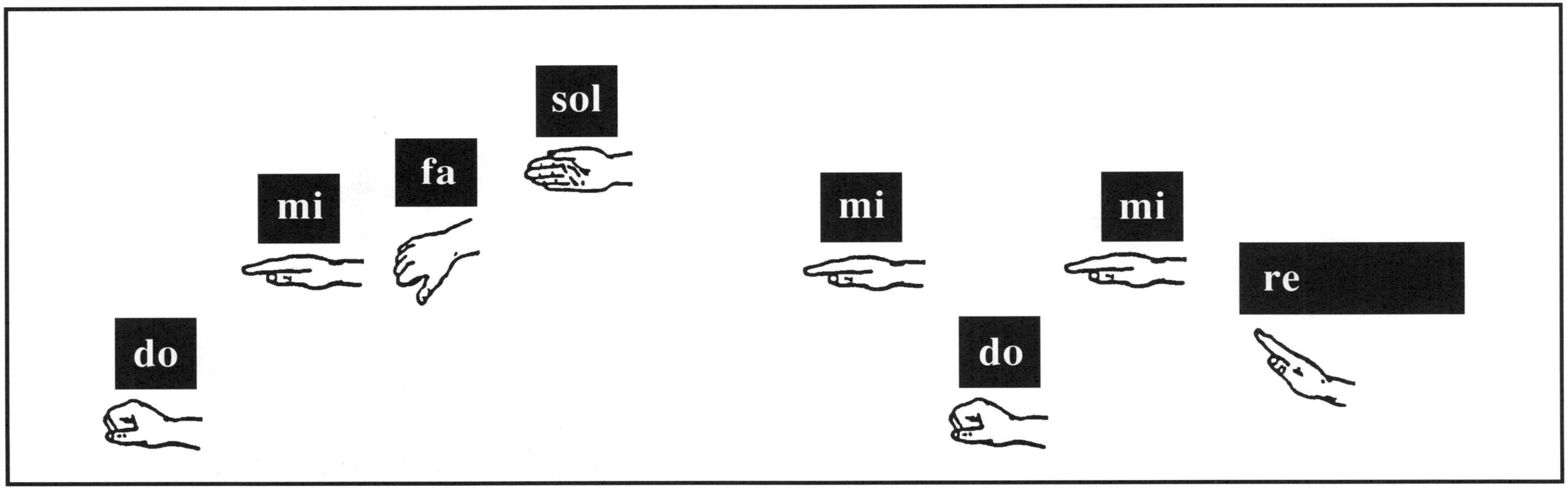

When the Saints Go Marching In

Keyboard and Guitar Harmony

Directions: Find these keys on the keyboard or chords on the guitar and accompany "When the Saints Go Marching In".

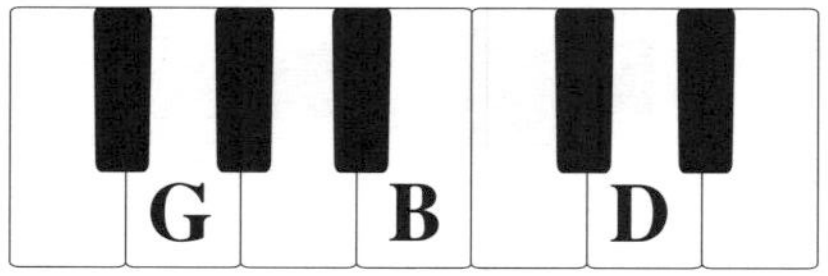

G

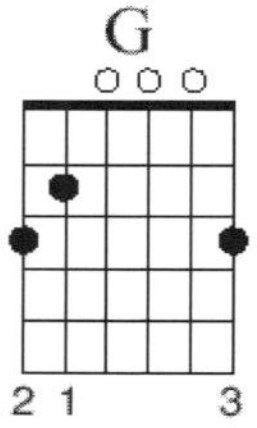

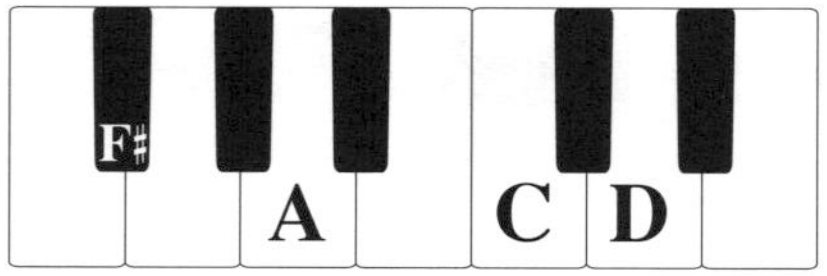

D7

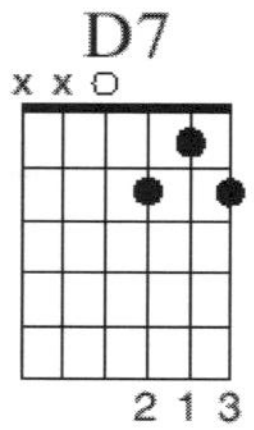

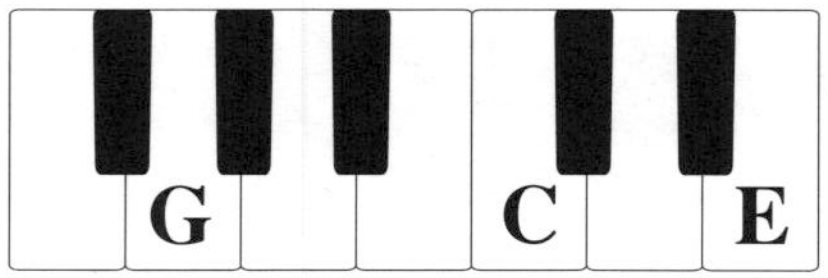

C

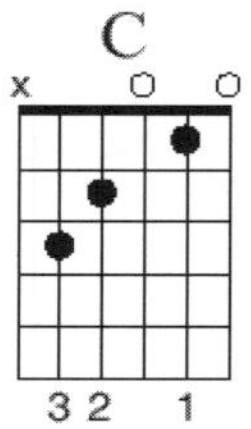

G G
Oh, when the saints _________ go marching in, _________

G D7
Oh, when the saints go marching in, _________

G C
Lord, I want to be in that number, _________

G D7 G
When the saints go marching in. _________

When the Saints Go Marching In

Recorder Duet

Melody by James M. Black
Harmony by Loretta Norgon

When the Saints Go Marching In

Adding Orff

SR = Soprano Recorder
SG = Soprano Glockenspiel
SX = Soprano Xylophone
AX = Alto Xylophone
BX = Bass Xylophone
BM = Bass Metallophone

Melody by James M. Black
Arranged by Loretta Norgon

When the Saints Go Marching In
(Adding Orff, cont.)

When the Saints Go Marching In

Sequencing Syllables

Directions: Cut these cards apart. Sing the syllables on each card and then arrange them in the correct order as they occur in the song.

do mi fa sol mi do mi re

---

mi fa sol mi do re do

---

mi re do do mi sol sol sol fa

---

do mi fa sol do mi fa sol

When the Saints Go Marching In

Partner Songs

When the Saints, Melody by James M. Black
This Train, Traditional Spiritual

Teacher Instructions

Yankee Doodle

Activity 9-1: Study Guide

Grade Level: 4-6
National Standard: 9

Objective
Students understand the origin and background of a song.

Materials
- Get America Singing...AGAIN! Volume 2, Singer's Edition, p. 49
- Student copies of 9-1
- Pencils
- Research materials or internet access

Directions
Open the class period by singing the song. Ask, "How many of you have heard this song before?" Facilitate a class discussion including any of the following:
- Where students have heard this tune
- What lyrics they recall
- What meaning they attach to the song

Distribute student copies of 9-1. Invite students to read individually or as a class as appropriate to students' reading abilities. Instruct students to work individually, in partners, or in small groups to find answers to the research questions. Encourage students to share their responses with the class.

Answer Key (Student Responses may include:)

1. *"Macaroni" quite possibly referred to an elegant style of dress, based on fine quality clothing and a practice of putting a lavish plume into the hatband. The English mocked the colonists' appearance saying that, simply by putting a feather in their hats, they thought they were sophisticated.*
2. *Answers will vary.*
3. *The English soldiers used this song to mock the colonists. They even sang it outside colonial worship services on Sunday mornings. The colonists, however, came to sing it as an American patriotic song, and it was performed at the surrender of Cornwallis at Yorktown.*

Activity 9-2: Comparing to Lucy Locket

Grade Level: 4-8
National Standard: 6

Objective
Students use appropriate terminology in explaining music and music notation.

Materials

- Get America Singing...AGAIN! Volume 2, Singer's Edition, p. 49
- Student copies of 9-2
- Pencils

Directions

Distribute student copies of 9-2. In partners, small groups, or as a whole class, follow directions on the page to discover similarities between the two songs. Sing the song, paying particular attention to portions that students have noted as similar.

Activity 9-3: Play Along

Grade Level: 2-4
National Standard: 2

Objective

Students perform melodic patterns on melodic instruments.

Materials

- Get America Singing...AGAIN! Volume 2, Singer's Edition, p. 49
- Transparency or student copies of 9-3
- Mallet instruments or keyboards

Directions

Distribute student copies. Help students sing the icons and lyrics. Allow practice time for students to learn to read the icons and play on bells or keyboards. Select students to play as the class sings the song.

Activity 9-4: Water Glass Chord Roots

Grade Level: 3-6
National Standards: 2, 8

Objectives

- Students play chord roots to accompany a song.
- Students understand connections between music and science.

Materials

- Get America Singing...AGAIN! Volume 2, Singer's Edition, p. 49
- Transparency and student copies of 9-4
- Water glasses, water, and metal spoons

Directions

Display a transparency of 9-4. Guide students to pour water into each of the three glasses to tune them to the pitches, G, D, and C. Ask "What are you noticing about the volume of water, compared to the pitch that we hear?" Help students learn to tap the glasses with the metal spoons to play the chord roots. Guide students as they follow the transparency and play the chord roots as the class sings the song.

Activity 9-5: Solfege

Grade Level: 2-5
National Standards: 1, 5

Objective

Students read syllables and sing a traditional song.

Materials

- Get America Singing…AGAIN! Volume 2, Singer's Edition, p. 49
- Transparency or student copies of 9-5

Directions

Display the transparencies or distribute student copies of 9-5. Assuming prior experience with solfege, assist students as they read and sing a portion of the song with syllables.

Activity 9-6: Recorder Duet

Grade Level: 3-6
National Standards: 2, 5

Objective

Students read and perform a recorder duet.

Materials

- Get America Singing…AGAIN! Volume 2, Singer's Edition, p. 49
- Student copies of 9-6

Directions

Distribute student copies of 9-6. Divide class into two groups. Assist one group in learning to play the melody. Assist the other group in learning to play the harmony part. Pair each student with a partner from the opposite group, and allow time for the partners to rehearse their duets. Encourage duets to perform for the class. Reassemble the original groups, and work with each group to help them learn the opposite part. Pair with partners again; allow time for practice and performances.

Activity 9-7: Adding Orff

Grade Level: 2-6
National Standards: 2, 4, (5)

Objectives

- Students (read and) perform simple instrumental parts while other students sing or play contrasting parts.
- Students create an arrangement.

Materials

- Get America Singing…AGAIN! Volume 2, Singer's Edition, p. 49
- Teacher copy or transparency of 9-7

Directions

Teach instrumental parts to students by reading or by rote. With student input, create an arrangement, layering instrumental parts to create a complex and interesting texture.

Activity 9-8: Transposing

Grade Level: 5-8
National Standard: 6

Objective

Students transpose a melodic fragment.

Materials

- Get America Singing…AGAIN! Volume 2, Singer's Edition, p. 49
- Student copies of 9-8
- Keyboards or mallet instruments

Directions

Distribute student copies of 9-8. Demonstrate the tonic chord and play the beginning of the song in several keys for the class. Invite students to work individually or in small groups to follow the directions on the page, and experiment with transposing as directed.

Activity 9-9: Follow the Map

Grade Level: 2-4
National Standard: 6

Objective
Students follow a melodic map and identify contrasting sections of a song.

Materials
- Get America Singing…AGAIN! Volume 2, Singer's Edition, p. 49
- Student copies of 9-9

Directions
Distribute student copies of 9-9. As you sing the song with the class, instruct students to follow the icon map. Discuss differences in the melodic "shape" of the A section and the B section. Help students discover that this song has two contrasting sections, A and B.

Activity 9-10: Variations: Souvenir d'Amerique

Grade Level: 6-8
National Standards: 6, 7

Objective
Students identify musical characteristics used in a theme and variations.

Materials
- Get America Singing…AGAIN! Volume 2, Singer's Edition, p. 49
- Student copies of 9-10, Transparency of 9-9
- Recording of "Souvenir d'Amerique" by Henri Vieuxtemps
- Pencils

Directions
Review "Theme and Variations" form. Distribute student copies of 9-10. Preview the map with the students. Review A and B sections of "Yankee Doodle" (9-9). Instruct students to make notes as they listen, to indicate what musical characteristics are most noticeable during each variation. Compare notes and listen again.

Responses will vary, depending on students' background in music analysis and also on the recording used. (This work has been recorded for violin and piano and for violin and orchestra.) Teacher may wish to encourage students to note when the violin is playing the melody, what kind of ornamentation or decoration is added to the melody, as well as dynamic and tempo differences among the variations.

Yankee Doodle

Study Guide

What are the roots of this song?

The exact origin of "Yankee Doodle" is uncertain. Some people believe that the first words were made up by a British surgeon, Dr. Richard Shuckburg, during the French and Indian War, as a way to ridicule the American troops. The British troops, with their precision and polish, sang Shuckburgh's lyrics and added their own, to poke fun at the colonists' ragged appearance and lack of formal training.

The source of the melody may have been a tune from Europe – perhaps a variation of an English nursery rhyme, "Lucy Locket."

Regardless of its beginnings, American soldiers and citizens came to sing the song frequently during the Revolutionary War. They created many additional verses, some of them poking fun at their own officers. They reversed the intent of the British, and turned it into a song of American unity and patriotism.

Since the 1700s, it is possible that as many as 200 verses may have been created and sung. Today, almost every American knows and can sing the song. The tune and lyrics have been included in classical and popular music.

Research Assignment

Find information about the following, and write your answers on the back of this page or word process on a separate page. Be prepared to share and compare your answers with the class.

1. What does "macaroni" mean in this song?

2. How many verses for "Yankee Doodle" can you find?

3. In what ways was this song used during the Revolutionary War?

Yankee Doodle

Comparing to Lucy Locket

Directions: Some historians believe that the words for "Yankee Doodle" may have been created to fit the melody of "Lucy Locket," a children's nursery rhyme from England. Compare the two songs, and decide for yourself.

Lucy Locket

Traditional

Yankee Doodle

Traditional

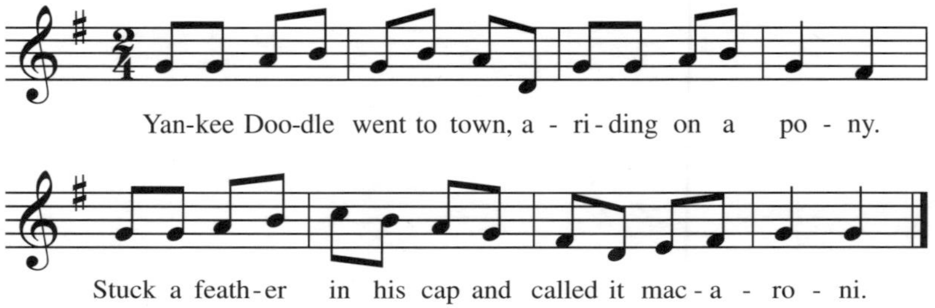

What do you notice about…

Length of the song?

Meter?

Melodic rhythm?

Write a paragraph about your discoveries. Include your ideas about whether "Lucy Locket" might have been the source of the tune for "Yankee Doodle."

Yankee Doodle

Play Along

Directions: Find these bells or keys on your keyboard. Play along with the song.

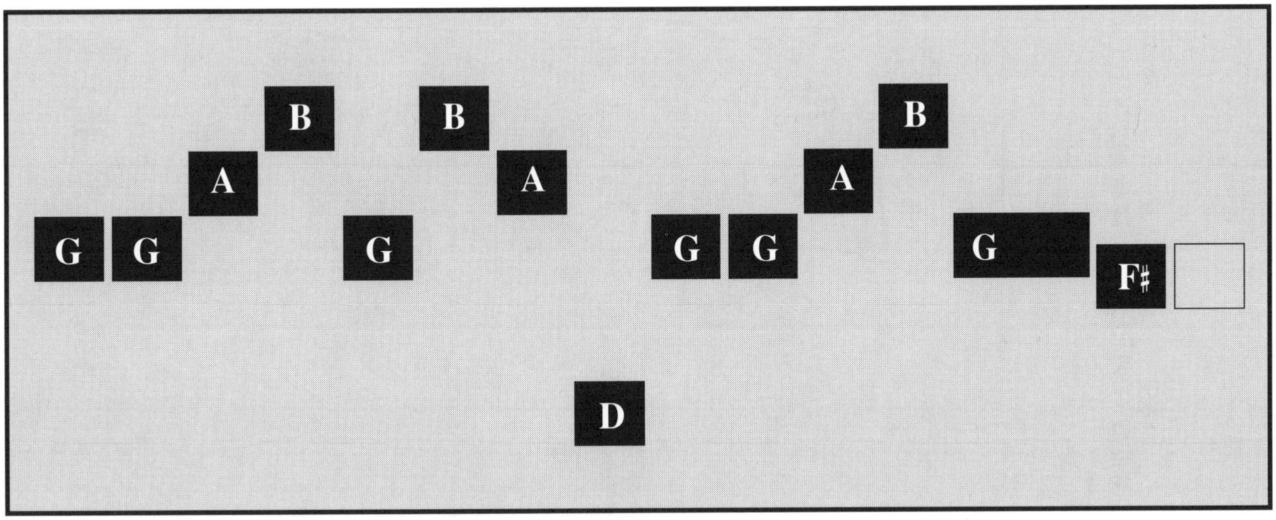

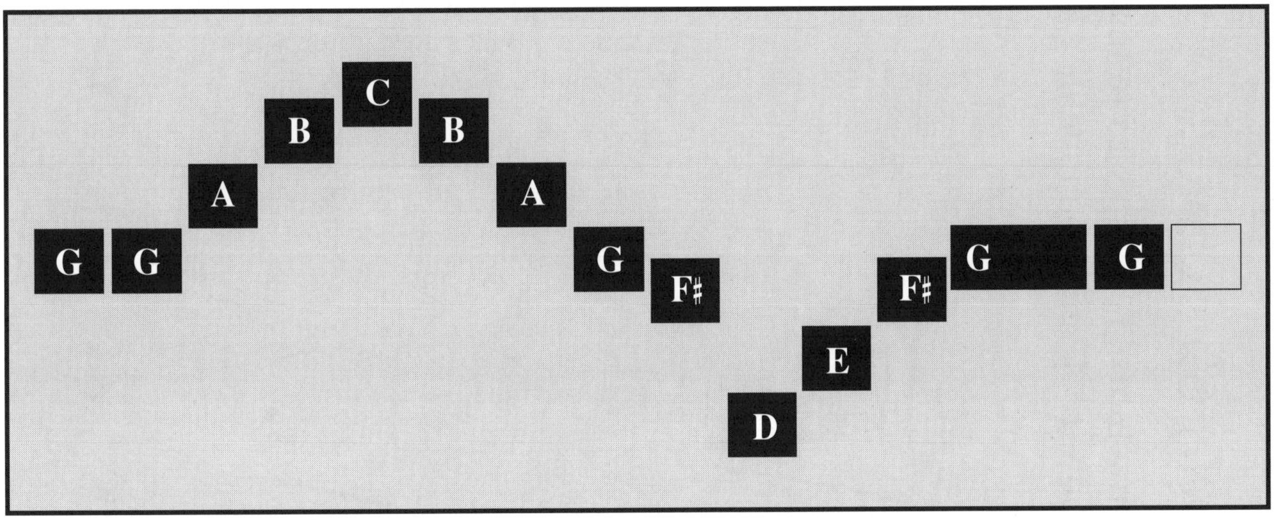

Yankee Doodle

Water Glass Chord Roots

Directions: Tune glasses to match each of these pitches. Sing the song and play the chord root accompaniment.

Yankee Doodle went to town a-riding on a pony,

Stuck a feather in his cap and called it macaroni.

Yankee Doodle

Solfege

Directions: Sing this melody using syllables.

do do re mi do mi re sol do do re mi do ti

do do re mi fa mi re do ti sol la ti do do

Yankee Doodle

Recorder Duet

Traditional Melody
Recorder Duet by Loretta Norgon

Yankee Doodle

Adding Orff

SR = Soprano Recorder
SG = Soprano Glockenspiel
SX = Soprano Xylophone
AX = Alto Xylophone
BX = Bass Xylophone
BM = Bass Metallophone

Traditional Melody
Arranged by Loretta Norgon

Yankee Doodle
(Adding Orff, cont.)

Yankee Doodle

Transposing

Sing the beginning of "Yankee Doodle" in the Key of G Major.
It begins on "do".

1. Play these pitches as you sing the beginning of this song.

The pitches in the Key of G

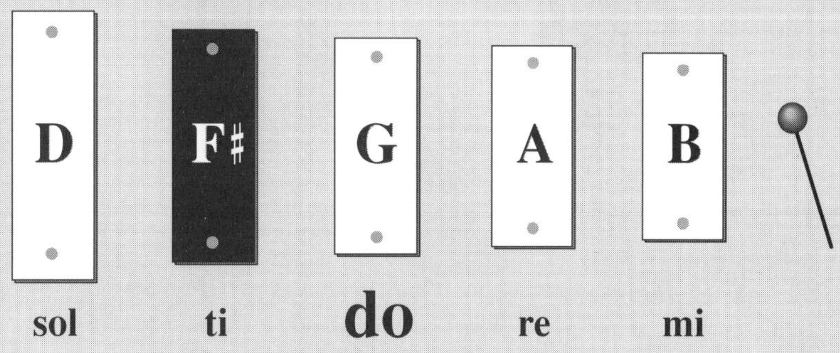

2. Find these pitches and play the beginning of this song in the key of F.

The pitches in the Key of F

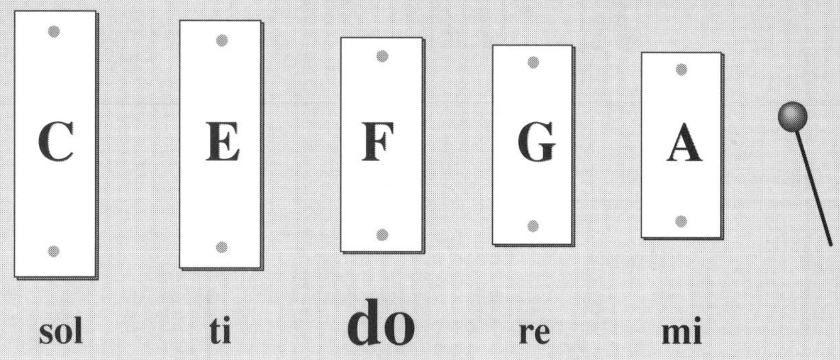

3. Using the same syllables, transpose the beginning of this song into other keys.

Yankee Doodle

Follow the Map

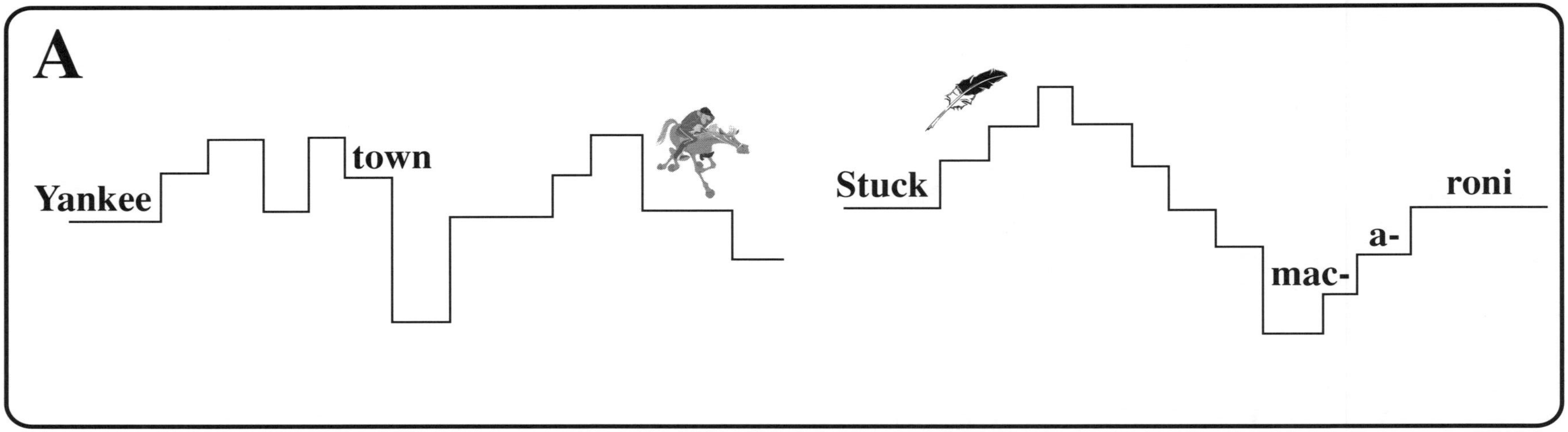

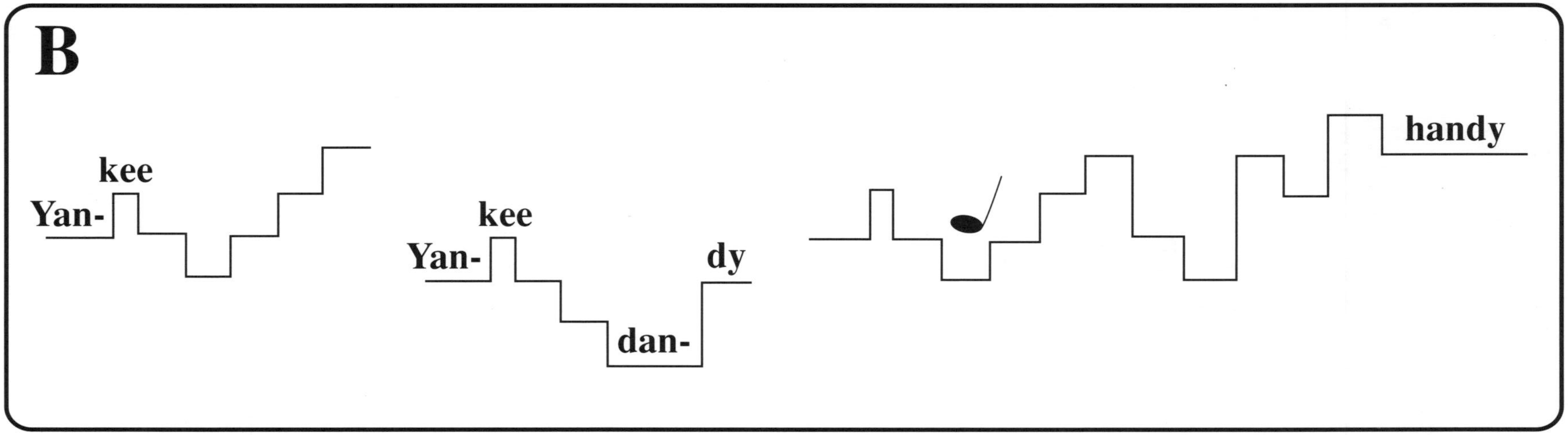

Yankee Doodle

Variations: Souvenir d' Amerique

Directions: Henri Vieuxtemps used the melody of "Yankee Doodle" to create a theme and variations for violin. As you listen, follow the map and make notes about what you hear in each variation.

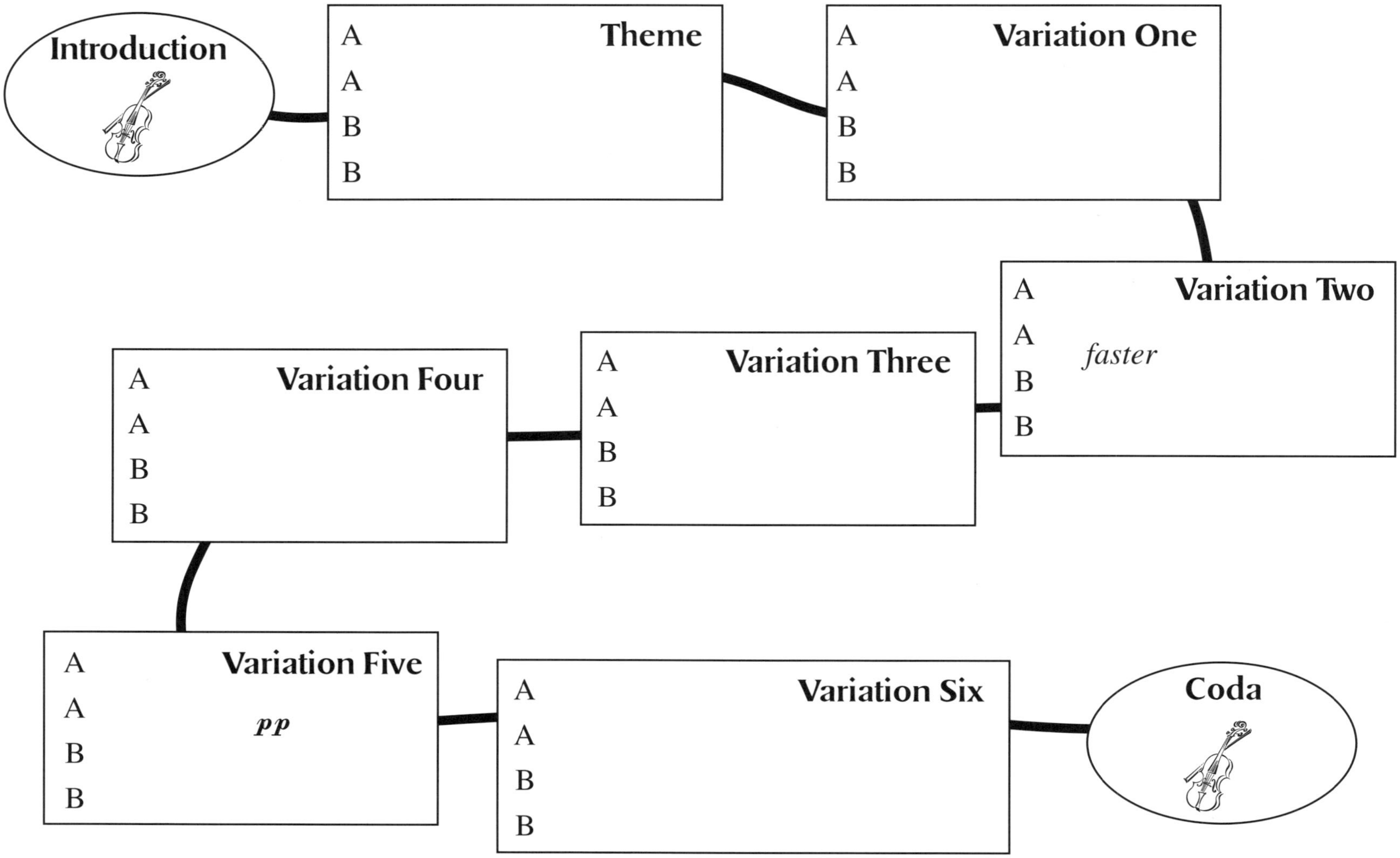

Teacher Instructions

You're a Grand Old Flag

Activity 10-1: About the Composer

Grade Level: 4-6
National Standard: 9

Objective

Students understand the origin and background of a song.

Materials

- Get America Singing…AGAIN! Volume 2, Singer's Edition, p. 52
- Student copies of 10-1
- Pencils
- Research materials or internet access

Directions

Open the class period by singing the song. Ask, "How many of you have heard this song before?" Facilitate a class discussion including any of the following:

- Where students have heard this tune
- What lyrics they recall
- What meaning they attach to the song

Distribute student copies of 10-1: Invite students to read individually or as a class as appropriate to students' reading abilities. Instruct students to work individually, in partners, or in small groups to find answers to the research questions. Encourage students to share their responses with the class.

Answer Key (Student Responses may include:)

1. *Vaudeville was theatrical entertainment in the late 1800s and early 1900s, consisting of a variety of singing, dancing, and comedy acts.*
2. *Living the vaudeville life, George was exposed to theater, music, and acting on a daily basis. He began performing and composing as a very young boy.*
3. *Answers will vary, but may include Little Johnny Jones, Forty-five Minutes From Broadway, Fifty Miles from Boston, Little Nelly Kelly, The Little Millionaire, Ah, Wilderness!, and I'd Rather Be Right.*

Activity 10-2: Research Project

Grade Level: 5-8
National Standard: 1

Objective

Students conduct a music repertoire research project.

Materials

- Get America Singing...AGAIN! Volume 2, Singer's Edition, p. 52
- Student copies of 10-2

Directions

Distribute student copies of 10-2. Instruct students to follow the instructions on the page, and discover, among people they know, which of Cohan's songs are the best known. Set a due date for the research to be completed. As students bring in their tallies, compile the grand totals and determine the best known of Cohan's songs among acquaintances of this class of students.

Activity 10-3: Learn the Lyrics

Grade Level: 3-5
National Standard: 1

Objective

Students sing a song from memory.

Materials

- Get America Singing...AGAIN! Volume 2, Singer's Edition, p. 52
- Student copies of 10-3
- Pencils

Directions

Open the class period by singing the song. Distribute student copies of 10-3. Define any unfamiliar words. Invite students to complete the page, working individually, as partners, or as a class as appropriate to students' reading abilities. Challenge students to sing the song from memory.

Activity 10-4: Betsy Ross

Grade Level: 4-7
National Standard: 9

Objective
Students understand the origin and background of a song.

Materials
- Get America Singing…AGAIN! Volume 2, Singer's Edition, p. 52
- Student copies of 10-4
- Pencils
- Research materials or internet access

Directions
Distribute student copies of 10-4. Invite students to read individually or as a class as appropriate to students' reading abilities. Instruct students to work individually, in partners, or in small groups to find answers to the research questions. Encourage students to share their responses with the class.

Answer Key

1. *The men who came to Betsy Ross' house with George Washington were Robert Morris and George Ross. George Ross was an uncle of Betsy's late husband.*
2. *It is said that Betsy Ross and George Washington attended worship services at the same church and that Betsy did some tailoring for General Washington.*
3. *The design featuring 13 stars in a circle was changed to a design featuring 13 stars in four staggered rows on June 14, 1777.*

Activity 10-5: Compose Your Own Flag Song

Grade Level: 3-6
National Standard: 4

Objective
Students compose within specified guidelines.

Materials
- Get America Singing…AGAIN! Volume 2, Singer's Edition, p. 52
- Transparency and student copies of 10-5
- Pencils
- Bells or keyboards

Directions
Display transparency. With the class, model the instruction and procedure for creating a short composition based on the lyrics provided. Distribute student copies, bells or keyboards, and pencils. Working individually, in partners, or in small groups, instruct students to follow directions as printed to create their songs. Allow time for groups to create and practice, and invite them perform for the teacher or for the class.

Activity 10-6: Melody Fragments

Grade Level: 3-6
National Standard: 5

Objective
Students read rhythm and pitch notation.

Materials
- Get America Singing...AGAIN! Volume 2, Singer's Edition, p. 52
- Student copies of 10-6
- Scissors

Directions
Divide class into small groups. Distribute one student copy of 10-6 and a pair of scissors to each group. Instruct students to cut the cards apart, shuffle them, read the melodies, and put the cards in the correct order to match the song. Encourage students to share their answers with the class. When all groups have the sequence correct, sing the song.

Activity 10-7: Patriotic Songs

Grade Level: 5-8
National Standards: 1, 9

Objective
Students understand the origin and background of their repertoire of patriotic songs.

Materials
- Get America Singing...AGAIN! Volume 2, Singer's Edition, p. 52
- Student copies of 10-7

Directions
Divide class into small groups. Distribute one student copy of 10-7 to each group. Direct students to follow the instructions and complete the project. Set a due date for projects to be finished, at which time each group will present their report and performance for the class.

Answer Key
Patriotism – a feeling of pride for one's homeland
Patriotic song – a song or hymn that expresses pride in and love of one's country
National anthem – official song of a county, performed at public events

Activity 10-8: Recorder Harmony

Grade Level: 3-6
National Standards: 2, 5

Objective
Students read and perform a recorder duet

Materials
- Get America Singing…AGAIN! Volume 2, Singer's Edition, p. 52
- Student copies of 10-8

Directions
Distribute student copies of 10-8. Divide class into two groups. Assist one group in learning to play the melody. Assist the other group in learning to play the harmony part. Pair each student with a partner from the opposite group, and allow time for the partners to rehearse their duets. Encourage duets to perform for the class. Reassemble the original groups, and work with each group to help them learn the opposite part. Pair with partners again; allow time for practice, and performances.

Activity 10-9: Partner Songs

Grade Level: 4-8
National Standard: 1

Objective
Students sing partner songs.

Materials
- Get America Singing…AGAIN! Volume 2, Singer's Edition, p. 52
- Student copies of 10-9

Directions
Distribute student copies of 10-9. As students are able to maintain the melody, introduce and rehearse the partner song. Divide the class into two groups. Sing the song with the partner song. Allow groups to reverse parts and sing the songs again.

You're a Grand Old Flag

About the Composer

American composer, George M. Cohan, was a singer, dancer, actor, songwriter, playwright, and producer. He began his life in show business early, when his parents, both vaudeville performers, added him and his sister to their act. Known as the "Four Cohans" the act launched his career for a lifetime in show business.

Among the many songs he wrote were "Yankee Doodle," "Give My Regards to Broadway," "You're a Grand Old Flag," and a famous World War I song, "Over There," for which he earned special recognition from the President of the United States. He was a major contributor to the art form known as American musical comedy, including costumes, dance, dialog, and, quite often, a theme of patriotism.

The movie *Yankee Doodle Dandy*, starring James Cagney, portrays the life of Cohan. The Broadway musical *George M!* is another tribute to the life of the famous American composer.

Questions to Research

1. What is vaudeville?

2. How might this have been a springboard to George's career in music and acting?

3. What were some of the many plays and shows either written by, produced by, or starring George M. Cohan?

You're a Grand Old Flag

Research Project

Directions: George M. Cohan was a famous United States composer. His songs are known and loved by Americans of all ages. Conduct a research project. Talk to people you know. Find out which of Cohan's songs are the best know among the people you know. If someone knows a song, ask him or her to sign your page. Tally the number of signatures for each title. Compare your chart with other members of your class.

Song Title	Signatures of people who know this song	Tally
You're a Grand Old Flag		
Over There		
Yankee Doodle		
Give My Regards to Broadway		
Mary's a Grand Old Name		
Forty-five Minutes from Broadway		

You're a Grand Old Flag

Learn the Lyrics

Directions: Fill in the missing words to complete the lyrics to this well-known patriotic song.

You're a grand old flag, you're a high flyin' flag,

And ______________ in peace may you wave;

You're the ___________ of the ______ I ______,

The ______of the ______ and the ________.

Ev'ry ______ ______ true 'neath the red,

___________ and blue, where there's

never a ___________ or ___________;

But, should auld ______________ be forgot,

Keep your eye on the ______ old flag.

Choose from these words:

acquaintance	heart
forever	beats
love	boast
white	emblem
home	land
free	brag
brave	grand

You're a Grand Old Flag

Betsy Ross

Our nation has a rich history. Our country's flag has an interesting story behind it also. Early in the days of the colonies, a lady named Betsy Ross earned her living by sewing for other people. She sewed upholstery. She also made clothing and flags.

George Washington and two other members of the Continental Congress came to Betsy Ross' house. They asked her to sew a flag from a design they brought with them. The flag had thirteen stars in a circle on a blue field. It had red and white stripes. Mrs. Ross agreed to make the flag.

Through the years, each time we've added states to our country, we've added stars to the flag. Our current flag has 50 stars, representing all fifty states. The fiftieth star was added in 1960 when Hawaii became a state.

Questions to Research

1. What were the names of the other two men who came to Betsy Ross' house? How did she know one of them already?

2. How did Betsy Ross know George Washington?

3. Look up the history of the flag's design. When did the pattern of stars in a circle change?

Project idea

Create a display or presentation that shows the original flag, the current flag, and some of the changes over its history.

You're a Grand Old Flag

Compose Your Own Flag Song

Directions: Find these bells or keys on your keyboard. Using short and long sounds for the words, make up a melody. Write your pitches in the spaces. Practice playing and singing your song. Perform it for your teacher.

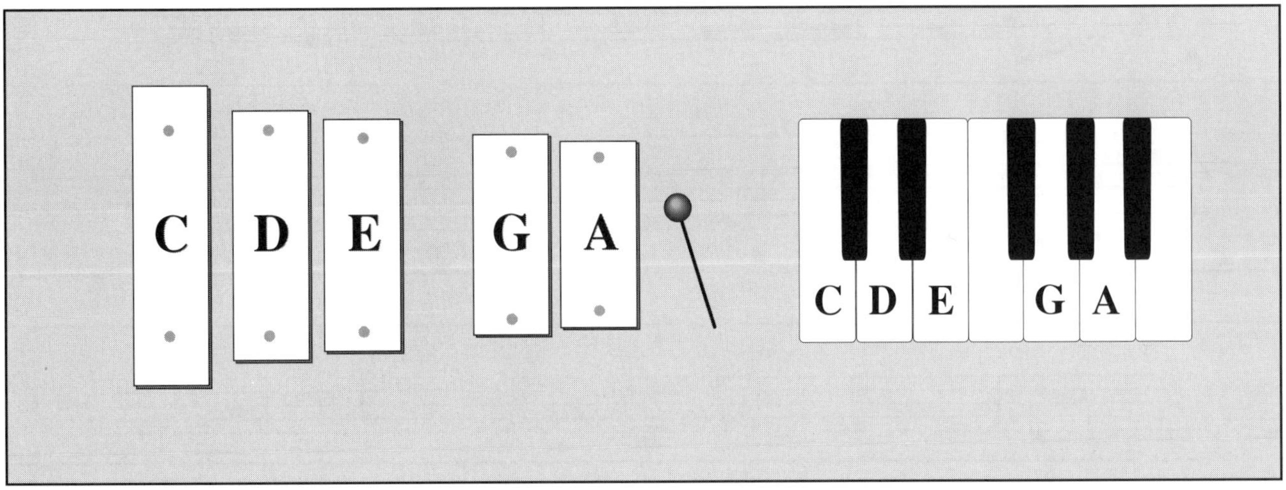

Wave the flag our coun - try's flag

For her - oes brave and true.

Spir - it of A - mer - i - ca,

Red and white and blue.

You're a Grand Old Flag

Melody Fragments

Directions: Cut these melody fragments apart. Mix them up and then arrange them in the correct order. Read and sing "You're a Grand Old Flag."

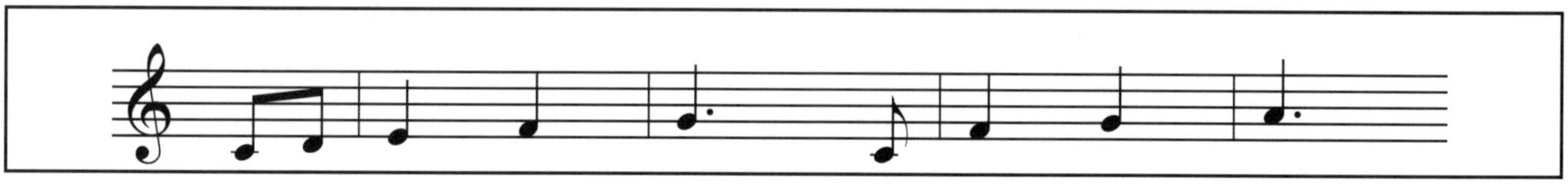

You're a Grand Old Flag

Patriotic Songs

Directions: Americans express their pride in and love of their country through patriotic songs. With your group, prepare a report on patriotic songs. Share your report with your class.

1. Look up and agree on definitions for the following terms and phrases:
   patriotism ______________________________
   patriotic song ______________________________
   national anthem ______________________________
2. Make a list of patriotic songs you already know.

____________	____________	____________
____________	____________	____________
____________	____________	____________
____________	____________	____________

3. Find two American patriotic songs that you do not already know.

   ____________________ ____________________

4. Choose one song from #2 or #3 above and prepare a performance and report. Ask for help from your music teacher or media teacher.

Title ______________________________

Composer ______________________________

Source (where we found this song) ____________________

Interesting things we discovered about this song:

-
-
-
-
-
-

You're a Grand Old Flag

Recorder Harmony

By George M. Cohan
Recorder Harmony by Loretta Norgon

You're a Grand Old Flag

Partner Songs

By George M. Cohan
Partner Song by Loretta Norgon

About the Author

With 27 years of teaching experience in classroom, choral, and instrumental music, **Loretta Mitchell Norgon** serves as classroom music coordinator K-8 for the Brainerd, Minnesota Public Schools. She also coordinates the Brainerd Teacher Support System, a formal induction program to support, assess, and improve the performance and effectiveness of new teachers. She earned the B.A. summa cum laude from St. Olaf College with a major in music education, and the M.S. as a graduate fellow in music education from the University of Illinois.

In addition to *Get America Singing Again - Strategies for Teaching (Set B)*, Mrs. Norgon is the author of seven other music education resources, and a contributing author for an eighth publication, the *Primary Teacher's Ready-to-Use Activity Program* (Parker/Prentice Hall, 1989). Her other publications include *Ready-to-Use Music Reading Activities Kit*, (1991), *One, Two, Three...Echo Me!*, (1991), and the *Music Teacher's Almanac* (1992), all published by Parker/Prentice Hall; and *101 Bulletin Boards for the Music Classroom* (1989), *Bulletin Boards that Teach Music* (1995), *Above and Beyond* (1999), and *Get America Singing Again - Strategies for Teaching (Set A)* (2001), all published by Hal Leonard Corporation. A regular columnist and contributor to *Music Express!*, Hal Leonard's bi-monthly publication for general music teachers, she created the column "Speaking of Standards" to provide classroom teaching strategies to work toward and meet the National Standards.

Under her leadership, Brainerd's classroom music department has been recognized as an exemplary model of standards-based education, and was awarded the Minnesota Alliance for Arts in Education Program of Excellence Award. The department's instructional materials, aligned with the National Standards for Music Education, as well as the department's online resources, are requested and shared with music educators across the country.

Mrs. Norgon is a frequent presenter for seminars and workshops for regional, state, and national education conferences. Active in professional organizations, her positions have included Classroom Music Vice President of Minnesota Music Educators Association and President of Minnesota Elementary Music Educators K-8. She teaches off-campus undergraduate and graduate level courses for music specialists and professional development courses for teachers of all disciplines, pre-K-12.

Throughout her teaching career, she has participated in strategic planning and development groups. She has served on the Commissioner's Task Force for Restructuring Education, the Minnesota Graduation Rules Change Committee, the Committee for Outcome Based Education in Music, the Committee for Music Assessment Development, the Frameworks for Arts Curriculum Strategies development task force, the Minnesota Handbook for Music Education review team, trainer and lead scorer for the Minnesota music assessment scoring team, trainer in Professional Development Planning for teachers, and Education Minnesota's "Teachers as Leaders and Learners" Project.

Mrs. Norgon was named Minnesota Music Educator of the Year in 1989. Other awards have included Brainerd Teacher of the Year, Minnesota Teacher of Excellence, Minnesota Honor Roll Teacher, Ashland Oil Teacher Achievement Award, Minnesota Professional Development Plan Fellowship, St. Olaf College Distinguished Alumna Award, and citations in Who's Who in American Education, Who's Who in the Midwest, Dictionary of International Biography, and the World Who's Who of Women.